FROM
JESUS'S
HEART
~ TO ~
# YOUR HEART

Dan Smith

ISBN 978-1-63885-310-7 (Paperback)
ISBN 978-1-63885-311-4 (Digital)

Covenant Books, Inc.
11661 Hwy 707
Murrells Inlet, SC 29576
www.covenantbooks.com

Contents

Introduction

People don't care how much you know until
they know how much you care.
—Theodore Roosevelt

God loves us unconditionally. When Jesus's love flows from his heart through our hearts and to the heart of other people, extraordinary changes happen in the lives of the recipients of his love. We are simply a channel, a vessel, a branch on the vine that allows that love to flow to others. Here are some heartwarming stories of love, faith, patience, kindness, humor, and character-building stories. I hope you will take these stories to heart and be the vessel that lets that love flow to a lost world, to your family, to your friends, to your neighbors, and also to your brothers and sisters in Christ. The rewards will be eternal!

Spiritual Encounters

The first spiritual encounter with the Lord was when I was seven years old. My family was attending South Baptist Church in Lansing, Michigan. Dr. Howard Sugden was the pastor. He preached a good message that I was a lost sinner, Jesus died for my sins on the cross, he is the son of God, he arose again, and he would wash away all my sins if I trusted him as my Savior. I stepped out into the church aisle at the invitation to go forward to pray and trust Jesus, but the aisle was so long; and there were so many people in that big church I ran back to my seat. At the evening service that Sunday, my parents went with me to the front of the church so I could pray with Pastor Sugden and be saved.

At the age of ten, I had another spiritual encounter. I was fishing off a bridge. There was a small river that flowed under the bridge. There wasn't much traffic on this road, so I felt pretty safe. I turned around and started to walk across the bridge to fish on the other side. When I got halfway across the bridge, I was right in the center of the road, and a car came flying over the hill, going so fast I had no time to get out of the way. Just before the car was going to run me over, I felt two hands push me right out of the way. The car flew by; I looked around, and there was no one in sight. An angel from the Lord had just saved my life!

I had another miraculous encounter with the Lord while I was attending college. I came home for the summer from South Carolina, where I was attending a Christian university. I heard that there was going to be a large rock concert out in the country on a farm that wasn't too far from my home. So I bought a thousand Gospel tracts to pass out at the concert. I asked my dad to go with me.

We drove off the paved road and went down a dirt road to get to the farm. We crossed over a narrow bridge that would only have enough room for one car to drive over it at a time. There was no way two cars could drive by each other across the bridge at the same time. We arrived at the gate that led to the field, and we stood right there and gave out Gospel tracts as the teens drove through the gate.

Because the teens thought we were handing out flyers about the concert, every car took a tract. Traffic was backed all the way up to the paved road. There were thousands of teens coming. We gave out the a thousand tracts in one hour. So we got back into my 1963 Ford Falcon and started driving back up the dirt road to the bridge. The cars were bumper-to-bumper in front of the bridge, on the bridge, and waiting to cross the bridge.

As I was approaching the bridge in my 1963 Ford Falcon, I pushed on the brake pedal to slow down. I was driving about forty-five miles per hour. When I pushed on the brake pedal, a brake line broke, and my foot and pedal went right to the floorboard. I could not stop, and I was going to plow head-on into the car on the bridge. Just before impact, I closed my eyes, anticipating the collision. I didn't feel anything! I opened my eyes, and I was on the other side of the bridge! All the cars were still in line, the car on the bridge was still there, but I was coasting to a stop on the other side of the bridge.

I said to my dad, "What happened?"

He said, "I don't know. I closed my eyes."

I said, "Look behind us. We are on the other side of the bridge."

Since he was with me, I know two people had just seen a miracle. Either God picked us up in one second and put us on the other side, or God let us travel right through those other cars in one second. I didn't feel anything go up, so my guess is we went through them without any collision, just like when Jesus went right through the walls to appear to his disciples. God is truly a God of miracles!

Let me tell you the effectiveness of giving out Gospel tracts. When I was in college, we had a man named Benito. He was from Brazil. He was part of a guerrilla communist gang terrorizing the countryside. One day while he was walking down a muddy jungle path, someone had dropped a Gospel tract on the trail. Benito picked it up, wiped it off, and read the tract. Right then and there, he accepted Jesus Christ as his personal savior. Now he was in college, studying to be a missionary to go back to the jungles of Brazil to win more people in the jungles to Christ.

Another man I'll call Bob was on a trip. He stopped to use a public bathroom. Someone had left a Gospel tract on the back of the toilet. So while he was sitting on the pot, he read the tract. The Holy Spirit opened his spiritual eyes, he saw that he needed Christ to have forgiveness of his sins, and he trusted Christ. He was now a deacon in a Baptist church. Never underestimate the power of a Gospel tract!

I had a spiritual wrestling with the Lord that was similar to the one Jacob had with an angel, except mine was in the spiritual realm, not the physical realm. I was in college, and it was my senior year. I was engaged to be married and I was about to graduate from college and my goal was to be a youth pastor.

I was reading a newsletter, and it was showing what was happening in the Vietnam war. There was an innocent villager who had his hands bound behind him. There was a communist soldier with a pistol to the villager's head. At the moment the picture was taken, the bullet had just entered the man's head from the side, and his face was contorting with pain. As I looked at the picture, it was like a voice came to my mind, and it was like the Lord was saying to me, *Will you go to Vietnam as a missionary?* It must have come, as I thought that poor man needed to hear the Gospel and get a chance to be saved before he died.

This was a total change in my plans. It wasn't at all what I was looking to do in the next six months. I was engaged to be married and finish college. And I wrestled with the whole thought that all of a sudden, God was asking me to leave my soon-to-be wife, my country, and my plans to be a youth pastor.

I kept thinking, *God, surely you are not asking me to do this?* And the thought would grow stronger in my mind, *Are you willing to go?* Well, not exactly right now when these big plans were just about to happen. I prayed about it every day, and every time I questioned this whole idea, the thought would be impressed on my mind again, *Are you willing to go?* Well, maybe not right now, Lord.

After two weeks of misery, wrestling with this whole thing, I said to the Lord, "Okay, Lord, I'll give up my wife and my plans that I thought you had for me, and I will go to Vietnam." Instantly my heart and mind were filled with peace. I was just released from this pressure that was upon me to go to Vietnam. I realized that God had just tested me to see if I would give up the person that I loved the most to follow him. Just like Abraham was tested to see if he would give up his son, whom he loved the most, for the Lord.

I prayed many times after that if the Lord really wanted me to go, he would provide the travel, the way, the money, all that would be needed, and then I would know it wasn't just a test but literally God wanted me over there. The prayers were never answered again in any way for me to go. It truly had been a test to see if I would give up for the Lord the person I loved most. I'm so glad I said yes to God.

The next spiritual encounter happened in 1976. My wife and I had graduated from college, and I was going to Indianapolis, Indiana, to interview for a part-time youth pastor position in a Baptist church. We were driving a 1971 Plymouth Fury I. It was a Michigan state police car that was purchased at a public police auction. It had the 440-cubic-inch engine, and it was super fast. We got about halfway to Indianapolis from Michigan, and my car overheated. We were near a rest area, so we pulled in there. I opened the hood, and steam was going everywhere. I didn't know anybody in Indiana; I was in the middle of the countryside, so there weren't any towns nearby. I was stuck here. So as I looked at the overheated engine, I prayed, "Lord, please help us."

Just then, a man walked up to me and said, "Looks like you need some help."

I said, "Yes, we do."

He said, "I think I have everything on my truck to help you." And he got his toolbox and started working on the engine. The thermostat went bad and caused my car to overheat. He took the housing off and removed the bad thermostat. He had a tube of gasket silicone to put the housing back on so it would not leak. He even had extra antifreeze to refill my radiator. He was standing next to me, and I was looking over the completed repair. I turned to thank him, and he was gone, his truck was gone—everything vanished. Praise the Lord, he had sent an angel to help me again!

Let me jump a little bit ahead in time and come back later. There are more stories of spiritual encounters. There are good spiritual encounters, and there are encounters with evil spirits too. I am going to share these stories to show you we can overcome these evil powers.

I was the director of Child Evangelism Ministries of Elkhart and LaGrange Counties in Northern Indiana. I established after-school Bible clubs at public schools. And it was legal to do so! The devil had brainwashed people into thinking that we couldn't have Bible clubs on government property, but that was a lie! In 1990, the US Supreme Court upheld the Equal Access Act. That law said, "If a public school has any after-school clubs, then they must also allow a Bible club!"

I was driving a 1980 Chevy Chevette. I was going from Elkhart County to LaGrange County to take care of some business for a Bible club. As I crossed the Elkhart-LaGrange County line, I came to a large hill that I needed to drive up. As I started driving up the hill, my car went *thud, thud, thud*. My engine was not firing on two of the four cylinders. So I could not make it up the hill. I turned around and went back over the county line.

As soon as I passed back over the line, my car was running fine. I turned around, went back across the county line again, came to the same hill, and my car went *thud, thud, thud* again. I could not make it up the hill. So I turned around and went back over the county line back into Elkhart County, and my car was running fine again. I pulled over, left the car running, and opened the hood to see what was the problem. I'm a licensed mechanic, and I did not see any mechanical reason why my car would misfire on two cylinders.

I prayed, "Lord, I believe a demon is messing with my car, and I pray in Jesus's name that you would remove all demonic activity from my car." I turned around toward that hill again. When I got there, my car went right up that hill with no trouble at all, and my car never acted like that again.

There was a lot of spiritual darkness in LaGrange County. There was a Wiccan coven there, and other Satanic opposition to my efforts to get the Bible programs established in that county. I also started a new Call-a-Story telephone line in that county. It was a telephone number children could call twenty-four hours a day, and they could listen to a three- to five-minute Bible story every day. There was definitely satanic opposition to that ministry. The machine that played the cassette tapes to play the Bible stories would stop working right. I would take a brand-new machine over there to LaGrange County, and the machine would not work right. I had checked it in Elkhart County before I brought it over, and it worked fine at the office.

I would pray over the machine, "Lord, I believe Satan is interfering with this machine. I ask in Jesus's name that you would remove all demonic presence from this machine and have it work right again." And bingo, the machine would work fine. Sometimes the cassette tapes would go bad, and sometimes a good tape would work at the office but not in LaGrange County. I would take the tape over to our CAS machine in LaGrange County, pray over it, and it would work fine. There definitely was demonic opposition to our efforts to get the Word of God to boys and girls in that county. But we overcame all the obstacles in Jesus's name!

There was a man in our area named Robert. He would picket churches on Sunday mornings, holding up signs that said, "Ban the Bible," "Jesus is not God," "Christians are hypocrites," and other nonsense. He saw my name in a newspaper article. The local paper had written a story in their religious news about me and my ministry. He called me and wanted to know if he could talk with me. I knew of his activity and his opposition to Christianity. I welcomed the opportunity to talk to him. He came and met me at my ministry office of CEM. He sat down, and we chatted about fifteen minutes or so. He was calm, friendly, chatting with me.

I said to him, "I would like to talk with you about Jesus."

He jumped up and started yelling. There was an expression on his face I will never forget.

He yelled, "If you are going to talk about that name, I'm leaving!" He rushed out the door and slammed it behind me.

I realized I had just talked to a man who was truly demon-possessed. Demons cannot stand the name of Jesus. It sent him into a rage.

I decided to send a follow-up letter to him, thanking him for coming and talking with me. I wrote the verse Revelation 12:11 in my text, "And they overcame him by the blood of the lamb." As soon as I typed that verse into my text, my computer went crazy. The screen flashed, the text jumped all over the screen, the computer went blank, and the entire letter I had just typed up was gone! So I knew it was demonic opposition again, and not a computer failure. The computer had never done that before and never did that again. I determined the devil wasn't going to win. I prayed, retyped the letter, printed it out, sent it to him, and I never heard from Robert again. There is power in the name of Jesus!

One day, my sister-in-law, Jane, asked me to pray through a house. There was evidence of demonic activity in the home. Lights would flash off and on; objects would move by themselves; a dog would appear to be running through the house, but there wasn't a dog in the house. The house had been used to house nuns from a local Roman Catholic church. So I told her I would be glad to come pray through the house. I started praying in the backroom of the house.

I said, "God, I pray in Jesus's name and in the power of his blood, remove any demonic presence that may be in this room. In Jesus's name, amen."

I did this, room by room. When I finished, I was standing by the front door, and there was a picture of a nun on the wall. It was an old black-and-white photograph of one of the nuns, but it gave me a creepy feeling as I looked at it. So I mentioned to Jane, "Why don't you take this picture out of here and get rid of it?"

So she did; she took it home. Her family had a fire pit in the backyard, and they were burning some wood in the pit. Jane decided to throw the picture of the nun into the fire to get rid of it. When she threw the picture into the fire, there was a loud explosion, *boom*, and flames shot up into the air. It was so spooky her son started to run away from the fire. So that nun was definitely involved in demonic activity in some way. In 1 Timothy 4:1–3, it says that doctrines of demons are "forbidding to marry, and commanding to abstain from meats." So in my mind, because there were doctrines of demons in that home, there were literally demons in that home. After the pray-through and the burning of the picture, there wasn't any more demonic activity in that home. There is power in the name of Jesus!

While we were living in Northern Indiana, there was a violent gang of thieves that lived in Elkhart, Indiana. They would go to surrounding cities in Indiana and Southern Michigan and commit their crimes.

There was a Laundromat located in Union, Michigan, right on US 12. It was kind of in an isolated area with not many other homes or businesses in the area. One day, this gang went to rob this Laundromat. There were three women in the business and a little girl, about five years old. For whatever reason, when the gang robbed this Laundromat, they shot all three women. Two of them died right in the Laundromat. The third one was shot in the head, but she survived. I met the third woman after her surgery. The top part of the left side of her skull was gone. The bullet had taken that part of her skull out. There was a big indentation where the bone should have been. She had brain damage but was recovering, and her final surgery wasn't done yet. I asked her what happened to the little girl during the shooting.

Another customer must have come in shortly after the shooting and called 9-1-1. The two women were declared dead on the scene. The third was unconscious and rushed to the hospital. When the police went through and searched every vehicle in the parking lot, they found the little girl hiding in a truck, and she was curled up underneath the dashboard on the driver's side.

The police asked her, "How did you get into this truck?"

She said, "A man took me by the hand, took me to this truck, and told me to hide there and stay in the truck."

There wasn't any man in that Laundromat. It literally was an angel or Jesus himself that took her by the hand, led her to the truck, and protected her from the shooting. It was a miracle!

Spiritual Battles

Our country's founding fathers believed and practiced freedom *of* religion, not freedom *from* religion! Like when the US Supreme

Court ruled in 1990 to uphold the Equal Access Act, we have the right to freedom of religion in the public arena. So I went to every school district in my county, and I met with the superintendents of each school system. Some of the school districts, we already had Bible clubs; some districts, we did not have any after-school Bible clubs.

As I met with each superintendent, I literally had to educate these educators that what I was doing was legal. Of course, they checked with their lawyers and found out that what I said was true. So most districts gave me permission to start the Bible clubs. One district I went to was very hostile to my efforts. He said he would not allow the Bible clubs in his district. I asked him if he had other after-school clubs, and when he told me that yes he did, I told him it was illegal for him to refuse to let me have our clubs. I would not take *no* for an answer.

I challenged him to look up the ruling of the Equal Access Act and to see for himself that what I was saying was accurate and legal. So he did look it up. He called me back into his office one day and was trying to make it as hard as he could to let me have the clubs. He told me that if he had one parent in his district complain about the clubs, he would cancel them. I didn't tell him this yet, but I did later—that if he did refuse me, I *would* sue him and the district. Sometimes, my friends, you have to have a backbone and stand up to evil, and truly there was demonic opposition to have clubs in this district.

So he gave me permission to contact each elementary school principal in the district. I did so, and I was very polite and spoke kindly to them. Most of the principals were also uneducated about the legality of the after-school Bible clubs. Some principals were very accommodating. A couple were not at all. First, they required that I have a teacher at their school that would sponsor the club. That seemed like a big barrier to get a public school teacher to sponsor a Bible club. But in every school, God supplied a teacher to sponsor our club.

Then the hostile principals told me there were no empty rooms available after school to have the club. Oh yeah, right, a whole empty building after school, and not one room was available?

I just said, "Well, please find one because you have rooms for your other after-school clubs. We need one too." I would not take no for an answer.

Then I was told that we could not advertise the club on the PA system or put up posters advertising the clubs.

I said, "Do the other clubs get announced on your PA system and put up posters?"

She said, "Yes."

Then I said to her, "Well, we get the same equal access."

And they would reluctantly comply. I would not take no for an answer.

The part I was concerned the most was sending home the permission slips for parents to sign up their children for the club. Again, I had to insist that if permission notes went home for the other clubs, then our permission slips went home too. Remember how the superintendent said if he got one complaint, he would cancel our clubs? Well, the response for the parents was overwhelming. Hundreds of parents signed their kids up for the Bible clubs. We literally sent home ten thousand permission slips, and we did not get a single complaint. Praise the Lord! God was breaking down every barrier that Satan threw up to stop us. God wants Christians with a backbone to stand up for what is right and to do it in his power and might.

One day, I was listening to a radio talk program on WOOD 1300 AM. An atheist in our community was trying to get the Release Time Bible club stopped in an area school district. Time Bible clubs are absolutely constitutional; they have certain requirements to follow to be legal, but they are legal. So many people were calling in with misinformation, including the atheist; I was not going to just sit back and not do something about it. So I called the station. I was put in contact with the person that hosted that program. He asked me if I would be willing to come on the air, live, and give what information I had on the subject of Release Time Bible clubs in the public schools. I agreed.

I went to the radio station. The day I was going to be on the air, I took Nancy and Jane, my sister-in-law, with me. Nancy would be with me in the station, and Jane would wait in the van and pray during the whole broadcast.

I brought a lot of material with me to back up my stand that the Release Time Bible clubs were legal. As we went on the air, the host started out by introducing a lawyer from a local law college to debate me on the air! He never told me I was going to have a debate with a lawyer. And this professor was a constitutional lawyer from the law school. So I just prayed for the Lord to fill my mind and mouth with the right words. The host let the professor talk first. We scheduled for fifteen minutes of airtime, and that was it for this debate. He let the lawyer talk first, and he spewed out his nonsense uninterrupted for seven of the fifteen minutes. I wasn't allowed a single word.

The station then went to a one-minute commercial break, and I said to the host, "When are you going to let me talk? That professor said a lot of things that are not true."

When we went back on the air, the host let me talk, and I stated unloading all the legal proof that the clubs were legal. I mean, with the Lord's help, I shot down every argument he had just given. When I finished, we only had two minutes left, and the host said the professor could have the last word. *No* way was I going to let that professor have the first seven minutes and the last two minutes as well.

He finished by saying, "So there is no place for God in the public schools." I didn't wait for the host to end the show.

I spoke up, and I said, "Oh yes, he does belong in the schools, and I totally disagree with everything you just said." I got in the last shot, and the host thanked both of us for being on the program, and we went off the air. The arguments that God gave me to promote the legality of these Bible classes were so strong our local Child Evangelism Fellowship rebroadcasted the entire debate on the CEF website! Praise the Lord, God got the victory. The station has never had me on again. I wonder why.

So many times God's people just surrender to the devil. We have lost ground to Satan, and it's time for us to reclaim what was lost. Just like the twelve spies who searched out the promised land, ten were bad and two were good. The ten said, "There were giants in the land,

and that the cities were fortified and too strong for Israel to conquer" (Numbers 13:28–29). They discouraged the people of God.

Joshua and Caleb, on the other hand, had unwavering faith in God and said Israel could defeat the enemy. They said, "Let us go up at once and possess it, for we are well able to overcome it" (Numbers 13:30). But the people didn't listen to the men of God who had faith in an all-powerful God. As a result, the adults all wasted away for forty years and died in the wilderness. In America today, religious rights are eroding away from us. We must stand; we must retake spiritual ground that has been lost. With God, we are able to overcome!

Here are some other examples of taking a stand for God and reclaiming rights that have been taken away. I wanted to have a Bible club in a city park. This is the same city where I had so much trouble getting after-school Bible clubs. So I met with the park superintendent and asked him if we could take our portable clubhouse called the Happy Day Express into a park to have a club.

He said, "No, we cannot because of the issue of the separation of church and the state. We could not have a Bible club on city property."

Again I spent most of my time reeducating people that their concept of this issue was in error. We have freedom *to* have a club, not freedom *from* having a club. America has been brainwashed on this issue. I found out that other organizations had been given permission to use the club, including a psychic club that used the park. So it was illegal for him to deny us.

I contacted the Christian Law Association. They are a wonderful group of Christian lawyers and defend Christian liberties. A lawyer there said the superintendent was wrong, which I knew he was, and that the CLA would represent our case to the park board. So our attorney sent a letter to the superintendent and the park board that it was illegal to deny us use of the park and they needed to give us permission, or legal action would be pursued. So the superintendent wanted me to come meet with the park board. In the meantime, our local newspaper got this story and printed an article on the park, denying our request. So now there was public pressure and a more hostile environment.

The day I met with the park board, the superintendent had made copies of the newspaper story and had passed them out to the park board just before our meeting, which didn't help at all. The board also had the letter from our attorney. So when the meeting began, I was asked to speak. I was very polite and not arrogant or condescending. I explained all I wanted to do was have a Bible club for the children in the park, and I was asking permission, not demanding it. The board was very open to letting me have the club, and they gave permission to do so, but it was based on an inspection from the fire marshal that the clubhouse wasn't a fire hazard. It's just like bureaucrats to throw regulations and paperwork at everybody. But we had to have an inspection, and it was all deemed safe. The issue was freedom *of* religion, not freedom *from* religion! We were fighting against spiritual darkness, and we needed to take the light of the Gospel back into that land.

> The only thing necessary for the triumph of evil, is for good men to do nothing. (Edmund Burke)

TRUTH PHOTOS BY CHRIS PUCALIK

Picture of the Happy Day Express

Next, I wanted to have a Bible club in a government housing project. One member of our church lived in an inner city-government project, and she wanted many boys and girls in the project to hear about the love of Jesus. I contacted the manager of the housing project, and I asked him if we could bring our Happy Day Express into the project, or use the public community building there on the property for a Bible club. Well, you know the answer I was given. I was told that we could not have a Bible club on government property. Again I spent a lot of my time reeducating people that their concept of the separation of church and state was flawed, and they had accepted the devil's lie of freedom from religion instead of freedom of religion.

I contacted the Christian Law Association again. They sent a letter to the manager and the board of the housing authority. Because the community building was open to other outside groups, we have the same right to use that building for a Bible club. It is illegal to deny us equal access. Well, after the housing authority reviewed the letter from our attorney, we were given permission to hold the Bible club. We decided to use our Happy Day Express clubhouse, and we brought it right onto the housing parking lot. We had ninety-five inner-city children attend that club. Many children prayed and accepted Jesus as their Savior. We also had a good missionary story of a lady that went into the dark jungles of Africa and brought the Gospel to the cannibals of Africa. The kids loved the stories. The club was held every summer there as long as I was the director.

I came into another spiritual battle that I was in a position to do something about it. A local school district, the same one that resisted my attempts to have after-school Bible clubs, announced that the senior graduating class could not pray, quote scripture, or do anything else religious at the graduation ceremony. Well, it just so happened that I had been elected president of our county's pastors' fellowship. As president of the group, I felt led to ask the other pastors to get involved and take a stand against this censorship of the senior class. Where the school board had this wrong, the school cannot sponsor any such religious speech nor does the school board have the authority to *prevent* such free speech but must remain neutral. The students have the right to student-led prayer, student-led scripture reading, etc. And it was illegal for the government schools to censor free speech of eighteen-year-old students who are legally adults at the age of eighteen.

So we released a public statement from our pastor's fellowship that we opposed all attempts to censor the senior's First Amendment freedoms. I contacted a local lawyer, and I contacted another lawyer from another state that was suing school districts who were censoring senior's free speech. Both attorneys agreed to attend the next school board meeting and asked for a retraction of the board's public statement of censorship of free speech.

We went to the school board meeting. The school board had an attorney from the liberal group, the American Civil Liberties Union. We were going toe-to-toe with these liberal attorneys that suppressed religious freedoms all over America. Our attorney submitted a resolution that the board take a neutral position and retract the public statement of censorship. The senior class also presented a petition, asking the board to allow them free speech. Out of 150 seniors, 143 had signed their opposition to the position that the school board was censoring their speeches. We submitted a statement from the pastor's fellowship of our opposition to the censorship of religious free speech. If pastors won't stand for public prayer, then who will? Parent after parent got up and supported the students' right to free speech. One ding-a-ling pastor from the Unitarian church got up and spoke in favor of censoring free religious speech, but the Unitarian church is on the wrong side of the Bible most of the time anyway.

The board flat-out turned down all the resolutions and petitions and requests of the parents and students. Right at the end of the meeting, this superintendent that had opposed my Bible clubs said to me sarcastically, "Do you think this activity on your part to oppose the school board will affect your Bible clubs?" The translation was, he was going to try to stop my Bible clubs.

I said to him, "If there is any problem, I will turn it over to these attorneys." He literally walked away from me like a puppy dog with its tail between its legs. He never bothered me again with the issue of Bible clubs!

Our attorneys needed me to get at least one student who would sign legal paperwork as the plaintiff to sue the school board. I got three brave seniors to sign the legal paperwork. The attorneys contacted the school board with the notice we were going to file suit. Now the board had a change of heart. They retracted their previous statement and now took the position that student-led prayers and student-led religious quotations would not be censored, and the board would take a position of neutrality—which is the legal and right thing to do. We won again, praise the Lord. But more importantly, the people of that community won, and God gave the victory!

God Builds Our Faith

My friends, do you have faith as small as a mustard seed? Do you really realize how much you can do for the Lord if you have the faith? Do you really believe nothing is impossible with God? Well, for me, it came in small steps to where I would be ready to take major steps in faith for the Lord.

First of all, I was working on my rusty 1963 Ford Falcon. A leaf spring in the rear of the car had broken. I was trying to get the rusty bolts out of the frame so I could remove the broken spring and put in a new one. There was one bolt that just would not come out of the frame. I heated the bolt, beat on the bolt with a big hammer, oiled the bolt, and that bolt would not come out.

My mother, Beatrice, had just returned home from the store. She is a woman of great faith. She saw I was working on the car and said, "How is it going?"

I said, "Terrible. I cannot get this rusty bolt to come out of the frame."

As she walked up the stairs to go into the house, she said to me, "When I get in the house, I will ask the Lord to help that bolt to come out."

I laughed at her just like Sarah laughed when the angel of the Lord told her she would have a baby in her old age. My mom went into that house—and literally thirty seconds later—that bolt came right out. I thought that was amazing! This was just a small step to get me where the Lord wanted me to have big faith.

I was a youth pastor for a Baptist church in Indianapolis, Indiana. I wasn't making much money at all. As a matter of fact, our income was so low we qualified to live in a government housing project. The church went through a mess of infighting. The church ended up in a big split, and the money to pay a youth pastor was gone. When I was told the bad news, I had a ten-dollar bill in my wallet, and that was all the money I had. I read the verse, "I have been young, and now I am old, yet I have not seen the righteous forsaken nor his seed begging bread" (Psalms 37:25). I had a wife and a new-born baby. Ten dollars wouldn't give me enough food or diapers for the baby. I took that ten-dollar bill, laid it on the couch, got on my knees, lifted the ten-dollar bill to heaven, and said, "God, this is all I have. You have not forsaken the righteous nor allowed the righteous to beg for food. So I'm just asking you, Lord, to supply our need. I don't have money for anything, and I'm not going to tell anyone but you, God, that I need help. In Jesus's name, amen." This was on a Sunday night.

Monday morning, I got a local newspaper and started looking for a job. "Pray as if everything depends on God, and work as if everything depends on you. He that does not work does not eat." I was look-ing for a job to take care of my family. That afternoon, a letter came in the mail. It had no return address. I opened it up, and there was fifty dollars in cash in the envelope. There wasn't any name, letter, or anything—just cash. Well, praise the Lord, he was already answering my prayer. I looked at the postmark date on the envelope, and it was mailed Saturday, one day before I even know I was going to need help.

I said to Nancy, my wife, "Take our clothes to the Laundromat." We didn't have enough money to buy a washer or dryer. She went to the Laundromat, opened up one of the machines, and there was a twenty-dollar bill lying in the bottom of the tub. When you only have ten dollars to start, that was the sweetest twenty-dollar bill I ever saw. In the meantime, I acquired a job as a security guard, but I would not get my first check for two weeks.

On Wednesday of that week, I got another envelope in the mail. Again, it had fifty dollars in cash with no return name or address. That night, we got a knock at our front door; here was a married couple that stopped by to see us.

They said, "We had it on our heart that you might need some help." They gave us forty dollars in cash and two paper bags full of groceries. Thursday night, we got another knock at the front door.

Here was another couple, and they said, "We thought you might need some help."

They gave us thirty-five dollars in cash and two paper bags full of groceries. The next evening, we got a knock at the back patio door. We had a very small backyard, and backed up to our backdoor, Pastor Aguilar had brought a pickup full of food!

We started carrying in the food, we filled every cupboard, we filled every counter space, we stacked the food on the kitchen table, and it was three-feet high. There was so much food that it was rolling off the table onto the floor. Yes! God does answer prayer, and yes, all I needed in times of crisis was to trust him. I would never have to beg for anything in my life. God would keep his word and take care of me!

This is a blessing my wife and I have cherished for forty-five years! And it really built up my faith to take God's word and believe exactly what he says! God's love, goodness, mercy, and care is everlasting. God used this experience to build up my faith for the upcoming building programs that I was unaware he was going to put me through.

God used another experience to build up my faith. I was teaching a fifth- to sixth-grade combination class in a Christian school in Niles, Michigan. I also was a leader in the Awana program at our church. I was helping another man named Barry to get the Awana circle taped to the gym floor. Barry was also a parent of a boy who was in my class. He owned a radiator shop in South Bend, Indiana, and he also hired me to work for his shop in the summers. I did a lot of auto AC work.

I needed a car really bad. I was praying for God to give me a dependable car with low mileage and good on-gas mileage. Notice I wasn't asking for a Rolls Royce or some expensive car, just a poor man's model car.

As I was working with Barry, he said to me, "Do you need a car?"

I said, "Yes, what do you have?"

He said, "I have a 1967 Rambler. It only has forty-eight thousand miles, it's dependable, and it's got a six-cylinder engine and good on-gas mileage."

I thought to myself, *Praise the Lord!* but I hadn't asked the price yet. I believe I only made twelve thousand dollars that year teaching the children in school. Christian schools pay far less than public schools.

So I said, "How much are you asking for the car?"

He said, "I'll give it to you for free, and I'll give it a fresh paint job too."

Oh my goodness, God used Barry's kindness to help me. I believe right while I was helping Barry with the Awana circle, God put in Barry's mind to give me that car. Praise the Lord. My faith was getting stronger with every answer to prayer I got.

During the next school year, I was getting sick, and the doctors did not know why. I would start getting sharp pains in my lower abdomen, and I would throw up until I went to the emergency room to get some pain shots. The doctors ran blood tests, this test, that test, and nothing showed up conclusively. Finally I had a fever of 104, was delirious, was in the hospital, and was very, very sick. The doctors thought I had scarlet fever. Finally, a doctor name Dr. Aquino, a doctor from the Philippines, said they would do exploratory surgery to see what was wrong. I asked him to please be sure to check my appendix, and if it looked bad, take it out so I wouldn't have to come back for further surgery.

I had a couple of bad experiences in the hospital, and I guess it comes under the category of building character: no pain, no gain. I was sick in the hospital a few times before the problems were final found.

I had been rushed to ER with terrible abdomen pain; they put me in a room overnight to run tests the next day. I was sharing the large room with three other guys for a total of four beds in this room. Diagonally across from me was a poor elderly man who had obviously lost a lot of his mind. Tony was given fast-acting medicine to clean out his bowel, but Tony was a slow-moving man. And sure enough, when the medicine kicked in, Tony did not make it to the bathroom, which was right next to my bed. But he tried. He left a long brown streak on the floor from his being all the way across the room right to my bed, and boy, did it smell. It was so bad, all three of us literally went over to the window, opened it up, and put our heads outside to get fresh air. So the nurses cleaned it all up. I had lost my appetite, and so did the other guys.

I was finally asleep, and I felt a tug on my arm that had the needle and IV pole. Tony had gotten up to go to the bathroom again, and he thought my IV was his walking cane. It was stretched all the way past the bottom of my bed: Tony was just about to pull the needle out or my arm. So I grabbed my IV pole and brought it back. Every time Tony went potty, he grabbed my IV pole. I could not get to sleep. I tied my belt through my bed rail, around the IV pole, and closed the buckle. Now my pole was safe, and now I could go to sleep.

Another time I had been rushed to the ER and was given a room, the old guy next to me said, "Do you have a broom?"

I was really confused at that request, so I said, "Why?"

He said, "I need to sweep up something in the bathroom." So I got up to see what he was talking about. He had pulled out his drain tube, and there was blood all over the toilet and all over the floor. I called for a nurse. They cleaned it all up and put him back to bed. I got up later to go potty, and he had pulled it out again. Blood all over again. So I called the nurse, and she cleaned it up. And then she came to me and said, "Here, take this pill."

I said, "What is it for?"

She said, "To put you to sleep."

What do you mean put me *to sleep? I'm not the nutcase.* I was literally afraid to fall asleep with that nutcase in my room. I just prayed to the Lord to watch over my body as I fell asleep with a nutjob next to me. I fell asleep, and when I woke up, I was still alive and Mr. Nutcase was gone.

The last memorable story was when I was in the hospital again. The doctors could not figure out what was wrong with me. So I was given a room for the night again. At 5:00 a.m., a male nurse woke me up. He had an enema bottle in his hand and a smirk on his face.

He said, "You are scheduled for an enema."

An enema at 5:00 a.m.! And to bet it all, he gave me a double enema.

The shift changed at 3:00 p.m., and the new nurse was making rounds. She came in to my room with another enema bottle in her hand! What, not again! And sure enough, she gave me a double enema too. Man, this was a bunch of crap, let me tell you. The shift changed again, and a female nurse came into my room with another enema bottle!

She said, "You have to have an enema."

I said, "Lady, I have had enemas twice today, and I'm all pooped out!"

She said, "What? Let me check on that."

When she came back, she said, "I'm so sorry. You were only supposed to have one enema, and the other two nurses did not mark on your chart that you had an enema."

You know what, those hospitals can get a guy killed!

Well, the surgery started with another doctor. Dr. Aquino was delayed with another surgery. My family and friends were all praying God would help through the surgery.

Just before I was put to sleep, a nurse next to my bed with her surgical mask on said to me, "Well, it's Mr. Smith."

I said, "Who are you?"

She said, "I'm Susan's mother."

It literally was a parent of a student I had in my class a couple of years earlier. I really felt God's presence was in that room when she said that.

Dr. Aquino showed up just as the first doctor was ready to sew me back up. He had removed my gall bladder. It was bad. Dr. Aquino asked if he had checked my appendix. The doctor said yes, but Dr. Aquino wanted to check it for himself since I had asked him to specifically to do so.

My appendix was inflamed and ready to burst. The other doctor had missed it and was going to sew me back up with a bad appendix, which if it had burst, I might have died in my weakened physical condition. Dr. Aquino probably saved my life that day.

Witnessing for Christ

Since I was saved at the age of seven years old, I have always had a strong desire to tell others the good news that Jesus loves them, died for them, and will save them if they believe and call upon his name for salvation.

While I was in high school, two of my friends accepted Christ as their Savior. One of my friends named Jeff was from a Roman Catholic family. Jeff wanted to get baptized and knew his parents would oppose the idea of being baptized in a protestant church. So one Sunday, Jeff snuck out his bedroom window, brought an extra set of dry clothes with him, and was baptized in my church. He is continuing to attend and serve at a protestant church today, praise the Lord!

I have a funny human-interest story about Jeff. While I was still in high school, my dad brought a horse. He was a reddish brown-and-white Appaloosa. He only paid seventy-five dollars for it, and we are about to find out why we got it so cheap. My dad and I drove out to see this horse we just bought.

It took a while to catch him; he kept running around the pasture so we couldn't get him. We finally got him in a corner, my dad held on to the halter, and I climbed up on his back. There wasn't a saddle or reigns; it was just supposed to be a chance for me to sit on his back. My dad let go of the halter, and this horse took off like a rocket. He was bucking and kicking, and I went flying about thirty feet through the air and was thrown into the dirt. My dad went back up to the previous owner and told him about this horse's actions.

The owner said, "That is why we call him Dynamite. No one has ever broken him!"

That was an important little detail that my dad did not get before he bought him.

So we relocated Dynamite to a friend's farm where he could be kept and boarded. It was not very close to us, so I only drove out there on the weekends to try to break and ride Dynamite. He was a very spirited horse! I would be with him all saddled up, get on his back, and off he would run, bucking and kicking until I fell off. But he learned a few tricks to get me off fast. He would take off at a dead run, take his front hooves, and stop instantly; and no matter how hard I tried to hold on, I would roll off him like a bowling ball thrown down an alley. He would also take off at a dead run and jump into the air and twist a ninety-degree turn while in the air, and again I would go flying off sideways.

One day, I decided to play a joke on Jeff and another friend I had named Mark. They had never ridden a horse before. Oh, boy, this is going to be good! So the three of us caught Dynamite, saddled him up, and I was holding his halter while Jeff and Mark were standing next to the horse. I said to them, "Why don't both of you ride him at the same time and you can hold onto each other?" I knew if I had them ride one at a time, whoever went first, the second rider would never get on Dynamite's back!

I had Mark get on first while I held the horse in place. He was bigger, so he was first in the saddle. Then I had Jeff get on the horse, and he sat right behind Mark. I let go of the halter, and Dynamite took off like a rocket. He jumped in the air, twisted sideways, and Jeff went flying sideways. Mark let go of the reins and took both arms and wrapped them around Dynamite's neck. I knew what was coming next. Sure enough, Dynamite was running full blast, stopped suddenly, dug both front hooves into the dirt, and ducked his head. Mark came off the horse like a bowling ball.

Because we couldn't ride Dynamite every day and could only do so on the weekends, our efforts to break him did not work. So my dad sold Dynamite for a dollar to women who had horses. She heard all about Dynamite's antics, so she did even try to ride him. She fed him, brushed his hair, rubbed his head, and treated him like a baby. Then one step at a time, she just put the blanket on him and babied him. Over time, she put the blanket on him and then the saddle but still did not ride him. Finally the day came to ride him, and he didn't give her any trouble at all.

She entered him in horse show competitions. Dynamite exceeded at it. He was especially good at stopping and turning. Yeah, I taught him that part! Dynamite won about three hundred ribbons. He was so trained by the reins she only had to barely touch Dynamite's neck and he knew which way to turn. He turned out to be a great horse.

How many times do we buck and kick against God? How long does it take for God to break our will? When, if ever, are we so submissive to God that just a gently nudge in any direction and we follow his will? I like this poem.

> Oh, break my life if needs must be,
> No longer mine, I give it to thee.
> Oh, break my will, the offering take,
> For blessings come when thou dost break.
> (Author unknown)

*****

When I was sixteen years old, I had a part-time job as a bagger/stock boy for Schmidt's Grocery stores. There was a little boy, about eight years old, named Tyrone that came to our store frequently. I nicknamed him Tyrone the Terrible. He would grab a shopping cart and rev it up like it was a car—*vroom, vroom*—and would take off running through the store. He would hit shelves and other customers in the store. The manager would send me to go catch him and get him out of the store. He would come back and do the same thing all over again.

One day, I caught Tyrone back by the produce counter in the store. I figured I would talk to him about Jesus. I wiped off the produce counter, picked him up, and put him off the counter. He was looking at me eyeball to eyeball.

I said, "Tyrone, do you know why you do these naughty things?"

He said, "No."

I said, "I will tell you why. When you are naughty, the Bible says that is what sin is, being naughty. And you need to have your sins forgiven, or you can't go to heaven." I explained to him how Jesus is the son of God and that Jesus died for him on the cross, and that if he prayed and asked Jesus to forgive him of his sins, Jesus would wash his sins away and give him a home in heaven. He was listening to me very intensely.

After I explained all that to him, I said, "Tyrone, do you want to pray and ask Jesus to be your Savior?"

He said yes, and right there, Tyrone asked Jesus to be his Savior while sitting on the produce counter in the grocery store. Now Tyrone was walking with me to go back outside and go home. We walked past one of my high school coworkers, and Tyrone looked up and him and said, "Do you have Jesus as your Savior?"

My coworker said no.

Tyrone took his finger and pointed right to his face and said loudly, "Then you are going to hell!"

Wow, Tyrone had it all right now, praise the Lord. We took him to a children's program at our church for a while. Over the years, I lost track of Tyrone, but I know one thing: I will see him again in heaven!

I fought the Lord about going to Bob Jones University. I did not want to go there. I heard it was a very strict Christian college. So I made my plans to go to Detroit Bible College. Evangelist Jack Van Impe graduated from there, and I wanted to go to that college too.

I applied there and got accepted. I applied for a number of scholarships, and it looked like I was going to get financial help. This was the summer just before I had my first year in college. I was ready to go to Detroit.

There was a pastor who had graduated from BJU, and he was pushing me to put an application in to BJU. I keep putting him off, and he persisted. So one day, I gave in to him just to get him off my back. I sent my application in and thought I was done with this pastor. Three days later, I got a letter from Detroit Bible College, and all my scholarships had fallen through. I was shocked. I do not want to go to BJU! Now what, does God want me to go to there? So I prayed about it and told the Lord, "May his will be done."

Sure enough, I got accepted at BJU one week before classes were to start and with a scholarship. I had wanted my will, but his will was going to be life-changing for me. So off I went to college. I did just fine there; it wasn't so bad. It was harder on the girls; they had more rules. But in every classroom, there was a saying by Evangelist Bob Jones Sr. One class had the saying, "Do right though the stars fall." As Christians, we are to stand for what is right, and if all hell and all the stars in heaven would fall, we should stand and stand tall. I would use the saying many, many times in the years to come to stand for the Lord!

In my junior year, I was in a car pool at Christmas time to drive back with other students from Michigan. We would share the gas expenses and help drive straight through to Michigan. One of the students in my carpool was a freshman named Nancy Blanchette. When Nancy saw me standing next to the car and realized that I was going to be in her carpool, it wasn't love at first sight. It wasn't even close to that.

She said to her roommate, "Oh great, I have to ride all the way to Michigan with him."

Wow, I did not know she thought that. I was short, too clean-cut, and maybe even a little ugly; she would not elaborate on that part. But I can read between the lines: "Oh no, a real homely dude."

As we started our long trip home, I found out by talking with her that she was homesick, and she wasn't coming back to college. Now my goal was to help this poor little freshman to come back and get her degree and not quit. I have a big sense of humor, and I joked and made her laugh all the way back to Michigan. So she did come back after the Christmas break and finished her final exams but was still going to quit.

Dr. Thurmond Wisdom was the dean of the BJU Institute. This program was in addition to all the other BA and BS programs. It was a three-year degree with special training in Christian service. He talked her into staying. But you see, one huge reason God wanted me at that university was because that is where I was going to meet my wife, and I just had but didn't know it yet. And neither did she.

She was the perfect match for me, and she would be right by my side in decades of ministry, through the good times and the bad ones too. She also was a very good ventriloquist. She had a dummy that was professionally done and painted by Maher Studios. The skin color looked real. And her talents and abilities were just what would make us the dynamic duo in our work with children, teens, and adults. And I would tell everyone I was her real dummy, and she put words in my mouth all the time. We dated for two years and was married in 1975. My life was truly complete with her, and all because God made me go to a school that I did not want to attend.

But backing up a bit, when I came home from college after my freshman year, I got a job selling vacuum cleaners called the little Green Pig canister vacuum cleaners. I was in a training class with about twenty other people who had also been hired. We were learning the sales pitch. But our trainer kept saying, "Jesus Christ this" and "Jesus Christ that" over and over again during his training sessions. It really bothered me that he was taking Jesus's name in vain so much. So I packed my shirt pocket with some Gospel tracts, and determined that if he keeps saying that, I was going to give him something to read that showed who Jesus really is: a Savior of the world.

So sure enough, he kept doing it again in the training sessions. When we paused for a ten-minute break, I walked up to him and said, "You talk about Jesus all the time, but I want you to read about him yourself."

I turned around, and all the other trainees were sitting there looking rather stunned, so I said, "Here, you can read about Jesus too." And I handed the Gospel tracts to all of them. Well, I figured after I did that I could kiss this job goodbye. And sure enough, the big boss called me into his office. There was the boss and the trainer I had given a Gospel tract.

The boss said, "That took a lot of courage to do what you just did. I think you are going to be our best salesman, and we will give you the first calls that come into the office."

I was shocked; I got a promotion, praise the Lord!

I was also attending a state community college there in Lansing in the summer of 1972. I had to take a couple of English classes that were required for my first year in college. So on the very first day of my English class, the professor got up in front of the class and said, "Today we are going to talk about the myths of Christianity." What! This is supposed to be English class, not an attack-Christianity class. This professor set out on each term to attack Christianity and to get Christians to stop believing the Bible and in Jesus.

So without waiting, I raised my hand and said, "There are no myths in Christianity." Well, it was on! We went into full-blown debate, and it was that way every day we had class. He would say something that wasn't true, and I would debate what he had just said.

About halfway through the semester, he said to me in front of the class, "How do you ever expect to pass my class with your views?" Wow, he was threatening to flunk me if I didn't agree with his baloney.

I said to him, "If I do the work, don't you have to at least give me a C for a grade?" Where is the concept of freedom of speech? Where is the tolerance these liberals always claim to have? Isn't there a difference of opinion allowed in academia? Or must we agree with liberals to pass their class? The whole class was waiting for his answer since he had threatened to flunk me in front of the entire class.

He reluctantly said, "Well, I guess that is true." We had to write a final term paper for the class, and I put right in the middle of my paper a personal note to him how he could be saved and trust Jesus as his Savior. I waited to see if he really did fully read everyone's term papers. So the next class, he told me to see him in his office after class. Oh, boy, here we go!

I sat down, and he said to me, "I read your term paper. I saw the personal notes you wrote to me. Are you trying to convert me?"

I said without any hesitation, "Yes, I am!" Guess what grade I got on my paper? Yup, a C, just like everything else I did in that class. Oh well, at least I passed, and I gave him the Gospel. I don't know if he got saved, but he sure got the message!

*****

Autographed picture of Danny Windsor as Flying Monkey

I led a flying monkey to the Lord. There was a man living in our area that was retired and working as a greeter at a Meijer's Store. He was in the original movie of the *Wizard of Oz*. His name was Danny Windsor.

When he was thirteen years old, he was a dancer and had been used in various roles, including a video of Elvis Presley. Danny was the jailbird holding the saxophone while Elvis sang the song "Jailhouse Rock." Well, Danny was near the set of the *Wizard of Oz*, and one of the men that was supposed to be a flying monkey in the movie showed up drunk. Danny was small in stature, and they asked him if he would be one of the flying monkeys. The metal harness he had to wear fit him perfectly, so he was literally one of the flying monkeys in the movie.

For whatever reason he settled in Muskegon, I don't know. But when I heard he had fallen ill and was in a nursing home, so I went to see him. I talked with him about what it meant to know for sure if he would go to heaven. I told him how he could pray with me and accept Jesus Christ as his personal Savior. He said yes, and he prayed with me and trusted Jesus for the forgiveness of sin. He then took one of his pictures of him standing with Margaret Hamilton, the wicked witch from the west, and he autographed it and gave it to me. It is something I will always treasure.

Witnessing on the Job

Because I have worked for a lot of poor-paying ministries, I have had to have secular work as well to help pay my bills. I only made $7.50 an hour working at a rescue mission in Grand Rapids, Michigan. At the same time, I was only being paid $50.00 a week to pastor a small church. But I accepted the ministries because Jesus said in Matthew 6:33, "But seek ye first the kingdom of God and all these things shall be added unto you." This means seek God first and he will take care of me, and it also means I may have to work more than one job at a time or even work in factories; but it's okay, I still put God first. It just burns me up when I hear a pastoral candidate say he won't take a certain church or ministry because it doesn't pay enough. That is not biblical, and it is not living by faith.

So by working in secular work, I can relate to the people in my church when I preach to them. I have been where they have been and worked the kind of jobs they have worked, and I can relate to them in my sermons.

I was working in a factory in New Paris, Indiana. It was July, and it was hot. I and another man named Dan were told to dig a ditch for a new pipeline. It was hard work, and we were both sweating in the sun. I was working quietly, and Dan wasn't working quietly. He was an ex-con, and he had a real bad family life as a child and ended up living in an orphanage. He was really cussing. Suddenly he stopped and looked at me and said, "Okay, what is it with you? There is something different about you. What is it?"

What a great lead into my opportunity to witness to him. I said, "Well, I am a Christian."

He said, "I thought so."

So I then gave him the full Gospel while we continued to work. I made it really clear for him to understand. We had to go behind a building to get more pipe from the pipe racks. There were different sizes and lengths on the racks. Dan paused and said, "What is that?"

And he got on his hands and knees and reached back under the bottom pipe rack, and he pulled out a balloon. There was a sting tied to it, and there was a note on the end of the string. Someone had taken a helium balloon and tied a Gospel tract to it, and it came down and blew underneath this rack. So he opened up the tract, and in big bold letters, it was John 3:16! He read the whole verse out loud.

> For God so loved the world, that he gave
> his only begotten son, that whosoever believes
> in him, will not perish, but have everlasting life.
> (John 3:16)

I could not hardly believe what had just happened.

So I said to him, "Dan, that Bible verse was sent from God just to you so that you would get it while I'm standing right next to you. God is speaking to you."

He looked at me and said, "You are spooky!"

I laughed, and then I said to him, "Dan, something similar happened with me before with another man, and three months later, he was dead. You need to really listen to that verse."

He said to me, "Man, you are really spooky."

We became friends, and I ended up conducting his wedding ceremony for him. I lost track of him over the years, and I don't know if he eventually got saved, but he sure knew God was speaking to his heart and mind when he found that tract.

*****

I was working in a factory again, and there was great big man called Big Jack. One year before I knew him, he had a bad Harley Davidson motorcycle accident. He bought a brand-new bike. He took it out on the highway for a ride. The factory didn't tighten up the front tire properly, and while he was speeding down the highway, the front tire came off and he had a bad accident. He had one leg that was permanently damaged, but he could still walk. So here he is working in the same factory as me.

I would go to lunch, and in the break room, I would bow my head and quietly pray for my lunch. He was watching me. So at my workstation—while I was working—Jack walked up to me, leaned over my shoulder, and said, "I can show you a way to cheat on your paperwork so it looks like you did more work than you actually did."

I said to him, "I'm not going to do that."

He said, "I didn't think you would, but I wanted to see what you would say."

Wow, I could have ruined my whole Christian testimony if I would have cheated on my paperwork. So now Jack decided he wanted to eat lunch with me in the breakroom. It was cute to see little ole me walking to lunch with this six-foot three-inch, three-hundred-pound man named Big Jack!

So when I found out about his previous accident, I told Jack the Gospel, and it was a good thing he didn't die in that accident. He didn't give me an answer but continued to eat with me.

Jack was a drinker. Almost every day after work, he would go to the bar and drink alcohol. One night, after drinking at the bar, he was speeding down a two-lane road, and a deer jumped off a small hill next to the road; and Jack hit it in midair with his van. He was going so fast it literally cut the deer in half, and the front half of the deer broke through his windshield, ripped the passenger seat right out of the floor, and ended up in the back of his van. Because Jack wasn't sober, all he knew was his windshield was shattered and he was covered with blood and hair, and at first, he thought it was his blood and hair!

Jack didn't come to work for a couple of days. Another employee told me what happened to Jack. When he came back, I wanted to talk to him again about the Lord because he was almost killed again, and he needed the Lord. Jack went to lunch with me again, and he was really quiet.

I said, "Jack, I heard about your accident. It's a miracle you weren't killed. God has given you another chance to be saved. You need to do this soon."

Jack did not give me any answer but gave me his phone number and wanted to know if he could call and talk to me sometime. I told him he could call me anytime. He did call a couple of times and just chitchatted but knew I was his friend and that trust was important. Jack did not make a decision at that time. I moved out of the area and lost track of him, but I know the Lord was speaking to his heart and mind that day in the lunchroom.

*****

I signed up to take a Dale Carnegie course on How to Win Friends and Influence People. There were people in the class from all walks of life, some professional and other people just like me. The very first day, we were told to come up to the front of the class and tell the class what was the most important thing to us. Well, the Lord is the most important thing to me; it's just having the courage to say it to total strangers my very first time they hear from me.

There was a man there in my class who was born and reared in France. He was a young adult in France when Hitler invaded France in World War II. He was a public figure, and so his name was on a list the Germans had of people to arrest. He had been tipped off his name was on the list, and so he was going across France to get to the west coast to see if he could get a ship to America before he was caught.

One day, he was in a small French cafeteria. There were two Nazi soldiers there in the café too, but they didn't know this Frenchman was wanted. One of the Nazi soldiers accidentally tripped over the French man's shoe, and the soldier was mad. He must have thought the Frenchman did it on purpose. So he took his rifle and put it right between the eyes of the Frenchmen to shoot him right there on the spot. The other soldier said something in German to this soldier, and the soldier dropped his rifle and walked out. My French friend asked someone in the café, "What did the other soldier say to the soldier who had the gun between my eyes?"

And a man in the café said, "The German soldier told his friend, 'Don't shoot that pig in here. Do it outside.'" The Frenchman's life had been spared. So he hastily made his way to the west coast of France and was able to get on the last boat to leave France before the Germans closed the borders.

This Frenchman said to the class, "I don't know why I was spared and able to leave France."

Well, there may have been a lot of reasons, but I figured it was because he was unsaved, and right now, it was for me to get up and give the Gospel in this class when it was my turn to talk. And that is exactly what I did: I gave a clear presentation of the Gospel and my testimony. I did such a good job that I won a speaking award that night in my class. I went up to him after class and was able to talk to him one-on-one. I told him one reason I believe that God spared him was so that he could get saved.

His response to that was, "I don't know about that."

In the meantime, another man came up to me and said, "I'm a Christian, and I should have said something about my faith too."

I said, "Yes, you should have said something too."

The irony of that was he was studying to be a missionary overseas. And I thought how ironic it was that he was going to me a missionary, and when he had a chance to share his faith, he didn't do it. As far as I know, he never made it to the mission field.

When my sons Kenny and Kevin were about ten years old, we would go to the local fairgrounds, and we loved watching the Demolition Derbies. So the boys and I decided to be in the demolition derbies. I would buy old GM station wagons and get them ready to drive in the demolition derby. That extra metal that station wagons have in the rear was very helpful in smashing other cards. It was a lot of work. Every piece of plastic, glass, headlight assemblies, taillights, and anything else like door handles that might fly loose had to be removed. The doors were welded or chained closed. The car battery was removed from under the hood, and we strapped to the floorboard in the front passenger side of the car. The gas tank was removed, the back seat pulled, and then the tank was strapped in the middle of the floorboard of the back seat area to keep it from being smashed or catch on fire.

One year, I was working on a 1984 Pontiac station wagon. When I removed the gas tank, the return lines from the mechanical fuel pump to the rear of the car had to sealed off. I accidentally missed one of the lines. When I started the car for a test drive, it was in the garage with the hood up. As soon as I started the car, gas spurted from that missed line right onto the exhaust manifold. The gas immediately caught on fire, and poof, I had a car fire in my car in the garage, which was also attached to the house. I could just see everything burn to the ground. The problem was every time the pump pumped, it squirted another splash of gas on the hot exhaust manifold.

So I yelled to Nancy, "Help, the car is on fire."

The rubber, grease, and belts were all on fire. She dialed 9-1-1. I grabbed a fire extinguisher as I was trying to put all the burning items out. I had managed to get the key turned off, but the fire was intense. So just as I tried to use the fire extinguisher, Nancy had grabbed the water hose, and she was spraying water; but it was right in my face! She was a bad shot with that hose. I'm trying to put the fire out, and I can't see anything but water.

I finally yelled, "Stop spraying water!" I got the fire out just before the fire engine arrived. My engine was really burnt. All belts, plastic hoses, spark plug wires, and wiring on the top of the engine was burnt black. So one piece at a time, I would replace what had been burned. I got it all done, and every engine cylinder worked good except one. Oh well, it ran pretty good on seven of the eight cylinders, and it was only going to be smashed up anyway; so all was good.

I did one more thing: I removed the differential plate on the rear end and welded the spider gears together. This gave the car positive traction, which was really good because the dirt track was always watered down and slippery before the derby began. We painted the number of the car on the side door, and the boys wrote their names on the sides of the cars and put other words but never any vulgarity on the car.

One year later, a Christian man was passing out Gospel tracts at the fairgrounds. The president of the fair board had him arrested for doing so and removed from the property. This really made me upset. I determined my car was going to be a witness for Christ at the demo derby, which was held on the fairgrounds. So with bright orange paint, I wrote "John 3:16" on the roof of the car in great big letters. And I was just going to see if the fair board would try to make me take it off, because I wasn't going to take it off.

I drove my car to the fairgrounds, went through the mandatory car inspection, and the inspectors didn't see the writing on the roof. I drove into the pit area, and there were 117 cars ready for the derby. I looked up, and a small group of people from the fair board were walking my way, so I was ready for what may happen.

The leader of the group was heading straight toward me. He walked up with the other board members and pointed to my car.

He said, "Is that your car?"

I was absolutely determined that I would not remove that verse, even if they kicked me out of the derby. I said, "Yes, why?"

He said, "We need a car for the president of the fair board to drive in front of the grandstands and greet everyone."

I could not believe my ears. Here are 117 cars, and they picked my car by chance? The Lord had directed them to pick my car; they just didn't know it. The board had not seen the John 3:16 on the roof, and this lady who would drive my car in front of the grandstands was the very person that had the Christian arrested for passing out tracts at the fairgrounds.

I said sure and handed him the key.

So she got in through the window of the driver's door; my doors were chained shut. And she drove over to the grandstand with my car and did a couple of small laps in front of all the spectators, and the verse was in big bright orange letters on the roof of the car. So she got done, brought the car back, and now the fair board wanted to know if I would drive the fair queen in my car in front of the grandstands too. Yeah, baby, I sure will!

She climbed in the front passenger window, sat on the window ledge with her legs in the car, and she held the door post and waved to the crowd as I drove by the grandstand again. Nancy had been sitting in the grandstand and didn't realize all that had just happened. All she knew was I was driving some young beauty queen in my car, waving at everybody, and she said out loud, "What is she doing in my husband's car?"

I took her back to the pit area. Not one official had seen the top of my car, but the Lord did; and he was getting his message out really loud and clear. I drove in the derby and had a smashing good time. I didn't win the derby, but I did win a battle for the Lord.

Building the Kingdom of God

Part 1

I took a new position as executive director of Child Evangelism Ministries in Elkhart and LaGrange Counties in Northern Indiana. When I started as director, the work was in decline. We had a few clubs and a few elderly teachers and low donations. I rolled up my sleeves and poured my heart into the work. The board had just sold our Good News Caboose, a portable clubhouse that was used for our five-day clubs, and it looked like a train caboose. The former director had not used the clubhouse very much. I was really unhappy that they had sold the caboose, so I asked the board if they would let me use those funds to build a new portable clubhouse. It would look like a train engine and be called the Happy Day Express.

Picture of the Happy Day Express

I used the new portable clubhouse extensively the first summer for our five-day clubs, a club which was held in various neighborhoods for five days, Monday–Friday. We took the clubhouse to homes, trailer parks, anywhere we could where there were children. This clubhouse was so successful that I asked the board to let me have another Happy Day Express built too. I would use that one for church VBS programs all summer.

Nancy was a ventriloquist and I did Gospel illusion tricks, and so we had good VBS programs for the children. I hired teens, college students, and even some adults to help me teach the clubs and conduct the VBS programs. Some of the teens were former sixth-grade students of mine that I had taught in a Christian school. We would run two VBS programs each week with five-day clubs being conducted all summer long as well. We were very busy. I would work from 9:00 a.m. to as late as 10:00 p.m., if the VBS programs were a distance away from the main office.

People heard of our work, donations were pouring in, and churches were adding us to their mission budgets to support us year-round. During the school year, we had Happy Day Clubs that meet once a week after school in some local schools in Elkhart and LaGrange Counties.

I had one club in Shipshewana, Indiana, that was mostly Amish children. We had about a hundred Amish children that stayed after school for that club. Then I had to help get them all transported home. We had a number of volunteers that helped. I drove a 1976 Ford station wagon. I could pile in fourteen children at a time to take home. That was before the day of car seats. I bought the car for one dollar.

When I would arrive at the Amish children's homes, their mothers would give me homemade bread, pies, cookies—man, that was good eating! We had a number of children trust Christ in that club. The Amish religion is a religion built on good works to get to heaven. So we would get the message to them through our Bible stories that it was faith in Christ to be saved. This was a wonderful experience I will never forget.

Our CEM office and bookstore was located in Elkhart, Indiana. But we needed to move the office to a more central location, and crime was on the rise in Elkhart. At one evening board meeting, a board member's car got stolen out of our parking lot. So the board decided we needed to move, praise the Lord.

We put our office and property up for sale. We were at the intersection of US 33 and US 20. We put the property up for sale for $115,000, and it sold in just a few days. A bank wanted that exact location. Now we had to relocate. When we sold our office/home on main street to the bank, we needed a place to live until we got our new office/home. The problem was everyone wanted us to sign a lease for at least a year, but we had no idea how long we would have to stay in a place temporarily. A man had an old—I mean, old—farmhouse that we could use. It was in really bad shape. I mean, some of the places we had to live in while serving the Lord were terrible.

This house had carpet that was soaked with cat pee. The toilet was rotting right out of the floor, the furnace wasn't working, and when we flushed the toilet, the water in the front yard came to surface because the septic field was plugged. A waterline by the washer was literally leaking water right onto a 220-volt outlet for the dryer. And the breezeway between the house and garage leaked really bad in a rainstorm, but we didn't know that room leaked at first.

Pam Pease and Anita Hochstetler came over to help. They pulled the carpet up and threw it outside. Then they scrubbed the floor with disinfectant. Pam fixed the floor by the toilet. We stopped the water from dripping on the 220-volt outlet. And we put all our CEM office equipment into the breezeway for our temporary office. When the first rain came, Anita was working in that office, and water started coming in everywhere from leaks in the roof. We had buckets and trash cans everywhere to catch the rain. Our golden retriever had gone into the basement. All of a sudden, she ran upstairs with an animal in her mouth. Nancy screamed, "A rat!" and took off running. I caught the dog, and she had a live opossum in her mouth. She had caught it living in the furnace that no longer worked.

This house was a real mess. But Nancy made the best of it, and she told our kids that this was just our temporary summerhouse.

That worked pretty well, because by the time summer was over, we did buy the new house and property by Eby's Pines. The house had belonged to the man who started and planted all those Christmas trees. He had died, and when the house went up for sale, CEM bought the house with plans to build our new CEM office right by the road.

Donations started pouring in, and the ministry was growing by leaps and bounds. We had a Call-a-Story telephone ministry. We had two telephone numbers where children could call and listen to a three- to five-minute Bible story for free. I started a new CAS line in LaGrange County, and the first year, we had a total of sixty thousand calls that came in to all three lines together. My volunteer staff had increased to a hundred people who help us run all our ministries, including an expansion of our mailbox club where children could get free children's Bible lessons in the mail. God blessed us, and we had more clubs, more VBS programs, more donations; but we still needed to build a new office/bookstore.

The board determined we had enough money to start a new building program; not enough to finish it, but enough to start it. And we made a commitment that we would not borrow any money but would totally trust God to send everything we needed to complete the project. First, we needed a contractor. An Amish man named Mel Miller said he would be our contractor, and all he wanted for the entire project was $1,000. Wow, what a blessing. Then Glenn Sharp of Sharp Steel gave us huge donations for the steel needed. David Bailey of Ira Mast Construction helped us tremendously. John Miller of Miller plumbing gave us discounts and help. Retired pastors, builders, and other men helped with the carpenter work. The ladies volunteered and made lunch for the men every day.

It's impossible to mention all the people and businesses that helped us, but God brought them and God brought the money. We had fundraising banquets, and we raised thousands of dollars to help with the building expenses. Mel Miller had such a good reputation with the inspectors that when they came to the building site and saw Mel, they just signed the permits and drove away. They knew he as an excellent builder. Other businesses helped us as well. Pam Pease and Anita Hochstetler helped with much of the building process, as they were office managers for us during the building program

We built a new office, bookstore, and a large attached building to hold our two Happy Day Express clubhouses. One day, Mel was finishing the drywall in the storage building.

He said, "Hey, Dan, come here. I want to show you something."

He said, "This is a God thing." He had started that drywall in our large storage building. He started at both ends of the building at the same time and then met in the middle of the building. He was putting in the last centerpiece of drywall. That building was so square and so precise that the last piece of drywall fit perfectly in that last spot.

He said, "It is very rare for a building to turn out so exact and square." I was so impressed.

I said, "That is wonderful, Mel. Great job." He was a wonderful contractor! When the building was finished, every penny had been supplied by God to finish the project! God said he would supply all our needs; he is faithful, and he sure did! We had a dedication ceremony and gave God the praise for this wonderful project.

And what is even more amazing is that God supplied all our needs, even when our treasurer was stealing some of the money for herself. I had some suspicions that there was some monkey business with the way the cash receipts were looking. Donation amounts were being blacked out with a black marker. Some records didn't look right. I took a bunch of the receipts over to a friend of mine who was a retired banker.

I said to him, "Look at these receipts and records, and tell me what you see. I will not give you any comments on this. I just want to see what you have to say."

He looked them over and said to me later, "There is definitely a problem with these receipts and records. Someone is doing something wrong here." I knew it, but I wanted an outside person to see if my suspicions were right.

I had been down this road before of someone stealing from a ministry while I was serving in that ministry. And it wasn't me that was doing the stealing. I was a youth pastor for a church in Niles,

Michigan. The pastor was stealing money from the offerings that came in, but I was unaware of it at first. I started getting my suspicions that there was something really wrong with this pastor. I was just about to go to the board, but he beat me to it. He trumped up some lies and false allegations about me and money. What irony that he is the thief, but he is accusing me on money issues—which was a bold-faced lie! He called me into a board meeting and had false charges written up against me without ever talking to me about any of it and without any of the deacons ever coming and asking me about it. I said, "What is this?"

The pastor said, "You are being fired, and here are the charges against you."

I looked at the list. It was really twisted. Here the man who was stealing was accusing me of money issues! And these so-called men of God, deacons, had never checked out anything the pastor said.

I said to all of them as I looked over the paper, "This is not true!"

One deacon said, "The pastor would not lie."

I said loudly, "He just did. And you men are going to find out the truth someday that this is a lie, and you are going to owe me an apology."

The deacons would not listen to me but listened to a liar and a thief. Well, he did finally get caught. He was stealing and his wife was altering the books, but none of those deacons had the integrity to call and make things right. It wasn't until fifteen years later that a different pastor had come across all this mess in some records of the church.

He called me to come there. He took me into the office where the pastor and deacons had falsely accused me, and he said, "The last time you were in this office, things didn't go so good for you, did they?"

I said, "No, it did not."

He said, "You have been exonerated. The pastor was finally caught that he was stealing from the church, and his wife was altering the books to cover it up."

I said, "Thank you so much for making this right for me. I really appreciate it."

But before I go any further, I want to tell you the rest of the story after this thieving pastor had fired me. There was another Christian school literally two blocks from my house. When we first moved to Niles, we didn't have anywhere to live. So the bad pastor and his son ran a renter's drug house, and they expected us to move into a duplex with a druggie next to us. I told him flat-out no.

We ended up living in a small home that was located right in the middle of a lumberyard. I have really lived in some rotten places. But God used that move to put us two blocks from another Christian school where I would end up working. There was a church and Christian school right by me, and Pastor Larry Whiteford was the pastor. He was a wonderful-loving pastor, and he preached good, and he was also a beautiful singer. He was called "The Singing Pastor," and he sang at some national Christian conferences. He made some records and sang every week at his church. Well, I went to see him to see if there were any openings in his school. I met with him in his office.

He asked me where I had just come from, and I gave him the name of the church and the name of the thieving pastor. I'm not giving those names; I have no interest in slandering another church or pastor by name.

He said to me, "Things probably didn't go very well there and so-and-so church, did they?"

I said, "No, they did not. Do you want me to tell you what happened?" I figured I would never be able to get a job in Christian ministry again if they called the former pastor and he told all those lies about me.

He said to me, "You don't have to tell me a thing. That pastor is mentally ill. You are hired!" Praise the Lord, I could not believe what my ears had just heard. Pastor Whiteford was also was a graduate of BJU, and I'm sure that helped me get hired too.

I taught a fifth- to sixth-grade combination class. One year, I had thirty-three students in that class. And I loved them dearly. I visited every student's home. It wasn't a school meeting; it was an

I-want-to-get-to-know-you-better meeting. The parents loved it, the kids loved it that their teacher would take time to come and see them at home, and I loved visiting in these homes. I learned a lot of interesting things in the homes that helped me better understand that student.

I had couple of boys in particular that needed my help. One was Byron. He didn't have a dad, he was the only child, and his mother asked me to be a substitute dad for him. Of course, I said yes. I took him to father–son banquets, I bought him a sixteen-gauge shotgun and took him hunting, I taught him how to work on cars, and I just spent time with him. When Byron was about seventeen years old, he was sitting on the couch watching TV, and he just fell over dead. The autopsy could not find a reason he did. God just took him home. I was the only acting dad he ever had.

Because I taught fifth- and sixth-grades, I had all the students for two years. They loved it, and I loved it. I poured my heart into those kids, and they loved me back. I had another special student named Robert. By sixth-grade, he had already had a number of heart surgeries. He had a plastic valve in his heart, and when he opened his mouth, you could hear the valve working. It would go *click*, *click*, *click*. His heart finally gave out when he was eighteen years old. It was really hard to see these children die before they ever go to adulthood.

I had another boy of special interest named Burt. He was adopted along with three other children into this Christian family. Burt had been abused as a baby; his mother took cigarettes and burned his little body. So he was removed and put in this nice family. But Burt had an anger issue toward women. I was the only male elementary teacher in this school. Burt was having trouble with his female third-grade teacher. So they asked me if I would take him for six weeks in the back of my classroom and help him transition back into the third-grade class. So I'm teaching fifth-, sixth-, and third-grades in my classroom. Burt and I got along really well; I poured my heart into this needy boy, and he responded well, went back into the third grade, and finished the year.

The next year, he was in the fourth grade with a female first-year teacher. She was told that if Burt was any trouble to come and get me. So sure enough, one day his teacher came to get me; Burt was causing trouble. My classroom was right next to fourth grade, and we had connecting doors; so it was easy to go next door. I told my class I would be back in a minute. The teacher had told Burt to go to the office because he was being naughty. He refused and was sitting at his desk. So I walked over to Burt, bowed down so I could look him in the face, and I said, "Burt, let's go to the office."

He told me no. He had never told me no before. So I took my left hand and put it under his right arm and said, "Come on, Burt, let's go." He took a swing at me with his left fist and just missed my nose.

So I said, "Okay, Burt, now we are going the hard way." I reached down, put him in a headlock, and lifted him right out of his seat. I keep him in that headlock all the way to the office, and he was swinging his arms at me all the way to the office. When I got there, I put him in a chair and went and got the principal. Of course, today if I did that, I would be fired. But back in the '80s, it was a different world; even his dad backed me up, and so did the principal. Because he was unruly and combative, I was justified in using psychical means to get him to the office.

Burt got the whipping of his life when he got home. I never had trouble with Burt again. The next year, he was in my fifth-grade class, and we had a good year together. I love and miss every one of those precious students I had back then. At the end of that year, the school was closed because of financial reasons. I was then hired at another Christian school just over the Indiana Michigan state line. I taught sixth grade there.

Many years later, Pastor Whiteford's wife, Bonnie, died. I went to the funeral. It was wonderful to see some of my former students. Scot Whiteford had been in my class, and he was now a fireman, and he had his uniform on at the funeral. His younger brother, Randy Whiteford, was only in about second grade when the school was closed. I had a lot of fun playing soccer with him at recess.

He was all grown up now, and he walked up to me and said, "I don't remember your name. All I remember is that I liked you." Wow, that was a wonderful compliment.

Another tall distinguished businessman walked up to me and said, "Mr. Smith, do you remember me?"

The last time I saw all those kids was in sixth grade, and they were all grown up now and were hard to recognize. I said, "What is your name?"

And he said, "Lance DeVries."

Oh yes, I remember him very well. He was a nice young boy. His dad had been a state trooper and was shot and killed in the line of duty. Some men had robbed a bank, and his dad stopped the car for speeding and didn't realize it was the bank robbers. When he walked up to the car, they shot him. I felt so sorry for Lance when he was in my class, and I went the extra mile to help him because he had lost his dad.

So before I get back to my story about the treasurer stealing from CEM, I want to finish this rabbit trail I started going down. I was now teaching sixth grade in a Christian school in Indiana. My first year there, we were about three weeks into the school year, and a mother of one of the girls in my class came in to see me after school. And she was mad. She came into the class and said, "I want to talk to you."

And I could tell she was mad by the tone. She closed the door and pulled a chair up to my desk and said, "My daughter has never had a man teacher before. Every day since the beginning of this school year when she gets home, she starts crying. What are you doing in this classroom?"

There was nothing bad going on in that classroom whatsoever, and I was not only puzzled but was starting to sweat because she was implying I was doing something bad to her daughter, which I was not!

I said to her, "Is Debbie out there in the hallway?"

She said, "Yes."

I said, "Bring her in here, and let's find out what is going on."

So cute little Debbie came into the classroom and pulled up another chair to sit by her mother.

I said to Debbie, "Your mom tells me every day after you get home from school, you start crying. Why are you doing that?"

And she lets out this loud, "Waa, I miss my sister."

I said to her mother, "What did she just say?"

The mother had a total change in her tone and attitude. She said to me, "Mr. Smith, I'm so sorry. Now I know why she is crying. Her big sister just left for college at the beginning of the school year, and when Debbie gets home to her empty bedroom, she misses her big sister." It had nothing to do with me! That mother had jumped to all kinds of wrong conclusions, but at least it was cleared up now.

About two weeks later, Debbie and her best friend, Holly, were up at the chalkboard working on math problems together. Holly, in a playful mood, took her chalk eraser and, with her right hand, smacked Debbie right on her left butt cheek. The white chalk left a big white square right on Debbie's blue skirt right on her butt cheek.

Debbie took her eraser and was going to hit Holly back, and I jumped up and said, "The Bible says to turn the other cheek." I could not have used that verse at a more unfitting time than I just did. Of my goodness, the whole class was busting out laughing. Of course, they thought I meant her butt cheek, but I meant her face cheek; but the cat was already out of the bag. I tried to explain to them what I really meant, but they weren't buying my answer. And I thought for sure I was going to see Debbie's mother again because of a comment about a butt cheek. But she never came in to see my about it.

One of my pet peeves at that school was all the favoritism that was shown to the staff's children. I treated them all fairly and all the same. One day, a man who was on staff and his son were in my class and stopped in to see me. He said his son was struggling in school, which he did struggle, but he had all passing grades, and the dad wanted to take home all my teacher answer keys to help his son study for his tests. Well, I made sure the students had all they needed to study including study sheets for the tests. So I told him *no*, I wasn't going to loan him the answer keys to the tests. What a dumb request. And if I did it for his son, it was only fair to let other parents have the same access to all the answer keys, and that would have been a real can of worms. I explained all that to him, but he was being unreasonable and wanted preferred treatment for his son.

So this parent went to the principal to demand that I give him the answer keys. The principal, who was a fair man listened to it all and sided with me and told the parents I would not have to do that.

Then I had another set of parents who were on staff and wanted a special favor from me. If they felt that their daughter was not ready for a test, they demanded that I give her an extra day above the rest of the class to take the test later.

I told them, "No way!"

She was a C-and-better student; she wasn't failing. If a student was failing, I would do extra things to help them pass.

We had a new principal just appointed that year to be the elementary principal. I won't give his name to slander him. But he was only a math teacher on the high school level and had never been an elementary teacher, and was totally unqualified to be the elementary principal. So the parents go to him, and he calls all three of us into his office. They explained what they wanted and why, and I explained to the principal that this request would surely cause all the other parents to get mad if staff kids are allowed extra days to take tests. And if I did this for one student, then I would have to do it for all of them, and that was a can of worms. I could not believe the principal's response.

He said, "Yes, you are going to do this."

And I flat-out told him, "No, I am not going to do this. The Bible is very clear about showing partiality, and I will not show partiality to staff kids. That would cause a great deal of problems with the other parents."

This principal confirmed that he had no business being a principal. After I tried to reason with him, he looked right at me and said, "Yes, you are going to do this, and you will tell me right now what you will tell your students." He was being so unreasonable.

I looked at those two parents, and I said to them, "Do you see what problems your request is causing?" And they did get it. So they told the principal that they were dropping their request.

He looked at me again and said, "If the parents had not backed down, I would make you do this." Oh no, he would not have made me do it, because I would obey the Bible and not show partiality. So I made up my mind right there: I would not be coming back the next year. I was not going to work under a bad principal like this.

So later that year, I announced to my class that I would not be teaching there next year, but I did not tell them why. One day after I told them this, I saw two girls passing a note. I would tease them and tell them if I caught their notes, I would take and read them to the entire class. Of course, if the note were embarrassing, I would not do that.

I said to those two girls, "Hey, I want that note."

They said to me, "Mr. Smith, you cannot have that note." Wow, now I really want that note. So I got up and went to get it. As I walked down the aisle, the girl passed the note to the next row. When I went over there, that student passed it to the next row. The whole class was in on keeping me from getting that note.

Finally I cornered one girl, and I was going to get that note. The class started screaming, "Eat the note, eat the note!" And she did. She put that note in her mouth, with ink and pencil writing on it, and swallowed the whole thing.

About two weeks later, those same girls were in the back of the room in a little circle, whispering and looking at me. I figured whatever was on that note was going to be today. About 10:00 a.m., I was teaching math, and I got a call over the speaker, "Mr. Smith, would you please come to the office?"

I put the chalk down and looked up; those girls were shaking their heads—yes, they wanted me to leave the room. So to tease them, I said, "We are doing math right now, and I can't come."

The girls looked at each other in shock. I was laughing inside; I did not know what was going on, but I was sure teasing them.

So about five minutes later, the office called me again and said, "Mr. Smith, would you please come to the office?"

I looked over at those girls and said, "I'm sorry, I can't come right now. We are doing math."

One of the girls then raised her hand and said to me, "Mr. Smith, can I go to the bathroom?"

I knew she just wanted to go to the office; I didn't know why, but she was trying. So I said to her, "Not right now. We are doing math."

She threw both of her hands into the air like, *Now what do we do?*

All of a sudden, there was the good principal, and he opened the door and said to me, "Mr. Smith, you are coming to the office."

I said, "Yes, sir."

He took me out and closed the door. My classroom went nuts. I heard them moving desks and running around.

He said to me, "Did you figure out what was happening?"

I said, "No, what?"

He said, "Your class has prepared a surprise going-away party for you since this is your last year here."

My heart just melted. Then he said to me, "When you go back in there, act surprised."

And that is just what I did. They had made a big banner to hang across the back of the room, "We will miss you, Mr. Smith. Good luck." And they had food, drinks, paper supplies, cake—they did a wonderful job planning it all. And that note that Danielle ate was the sign-up list for what every student was supposed to bring, and that is why they didn't want me to see it. And the best gift of all, they gave me a picture of a nice buck, and they all signed their names on the back of the picture. I have the picture in my house today, thirty years later, and I will always treasure that class.

Picture of the deer picture

But I had one more goal to do before I left this school. When I would bring in wild game to the lunchroom, most of the teachers would not even try it. So I figured a way to play my last trick on them.

I shot two woodchucks. Woodchucks in Indiana are plentiful, and farmers hate them because they dig big holes, eat crops, and cause damage to foundations that they dig under. I brought the woodchucks home and put them in a Crock-Pot to cook. The meat was really tender, and I took all the bones out so the teachers would not be able to tell what kind of animal was in the pot. Nancy put some good spices in there, and it looked and smelled like chuck roast.

I took the Crock-Pot to school and set it up in the teacher's breakroom. I put a big stack of white bread next to it and put a sign up that said, "Hot chuck sandwiches," then turned on the crockpot, and the smell filled the room. I purposely waited ten minutes after lunch started to see if all of them were eating. Sure enough, when I went into the lunchroom, they were all eating the hot chuck sandwiches. The science teacher was the only one who knew it was woodchuck. So he walks in the lunchroom, and he says to them all, "Are you all enjoying eating that?"

And one of the said, "Yes, why?"

And he said, "Dan brought in that food."

Instantly they started pushing the plate away from them and said at the same time, "What is this?"

I said, "Just what the sign says. 'Hot chuck sandwiches.'"

And the science teacher says, "Yeah, woodchuck!"

Oh yeah, I got them all! One teacher named Drew had his fork halfway up to his mouth and just stopped, and he was looking at the meat.

I said, "Drew, what's the matter?"

He says, "My stomach says it's good, but my mind says it isn't."

Since I was leaving this school, I might as well leave with something they would never forget!

I took the rest of the woodchuck back to my sixth-grade class and asked them if they would like some woodchuck. Many of them did. I would have parents say to me at parent–teacher conferences sometimes, "My kids come home from school with the craziest stories from school."

And I would say to them, "Sometimes your kids come to school from home with the craziest stories too." And the parents would shut right up.

*****

Now that I'm finished going down some rabbit trails, I'll get back to this story about the treasurer stealing. Since I had been with one ministry where there was a thief, I'm going to make sure I don't get blamed for anything again at this ministry! I went to the board and tried to tell them, and they would not listen to me. The devil got his nose in the door and started causing all kinds of stress, internal fighting, and downright lies. Again, I'm not giving names so no one is slandered.

A lot of the issues centered around a new assistant director that had been hired. I took a pastor with me to talk to her to try to get the problems solved, and she refused to talk with us. She caused all kinds of problems in this ministry, and again the board would not listen. Here we completed a brand-new office/bookstore, and the devil was trying to tear it apart from the inside. I wasn't going to get caught up in a mess like I did before where the pastor had been stealing, so I resigned.

About six months after I resigned, the new director called me and said, "Well, you were right, the treasurer was stealing money from this ministry. Someone broke the password in her computer, and we found proof of what she had been doing."

When I resigned from this ministry, Dann and Pam Pease, with some other folks had a very nice going-away open house for us. The people were very gracious and kind for all the work we had done. And it was by God's grace that so much had been accomplished. A collection was taken by all the people who came, and they literally gave us five thousand dollars as a thank-you gift. We appreciated that so much! It really helped us to get our new home in Michigan. I had poured the love of Jesus into the lives of everyone connected to this ministry, and the love flowed right back!

Police Chaplain

While I was living in Indiana working as the director of CEM, I applied to be a ride along chaplain for a local police department. I was accepted, and I rode on third shift. It was the shift with the new police officers, and there was always something happening in the middle of the night where a chaplain could help. So I really enjoyed riding with these officers. I had a name tag and a jacket that said "Chaplain" on it so I could be easily identified. A criminal that had been arrested one night looked at my jacket, and he called me "chaplain pig."

One night, there was a big fight in a park right in the inner city where crime was so bad. I was riding with an officer, and we pulled up to the perimeter of the park; and there was at least fifty people in that group. Some were fighting, and some were spectators. Two more squad cars pulled up to help. The K9 squad car pulled up, and that dog was really barking. One man on the perimeter of the fight yelled out just one word, and the whole fight was over. He yelled out, "Dog!" That whole crowd took off running, and the fight was over. A lot of crime can be deterred with a police dog.

One night, I rode with the K9 officer. He turned on his siren to go to a call, and the dog went nuts, barking its head off. I said to the officer, "Does the siren make him go off like that?"

He said, "No, he likes the taste of hot blood, and when I turn the siren on, he wants to bite somebody!" Well, I never asked that question again. The police department had about nine thousand dollars invested into each dog. The dog may get five years of service, but they are worth every penny.

One night when I was on duty, the K9 officer pulled over a speeding car. The report came back the car was stolen. So the officer got out of the car with the dog and ordered the man out of the car. He was a very large Black man, and he was high on drugs.

As the man got out of the car, he had his back to the officer, but he had a loaded gun in his waistband. As the officer approached, the man pulled the gun and whirled around to shoot the officer. When the dog saw the gun, he immediately lunged forward and bit down hard on the man's arm. But he was so full of drugs, he kept pulling the trigger, trying to shoot the dog and the officer.

The officer had to fire multiple rounds into this drug-crazed man, and finally the man went down. As I drove up in a squad car with another officer, the man who was shot was being rolled over to see the extent of his wounds. He let out a loud moan; he was still alive, so the officers went into emergency mode to try to save his life. He lived but went to prison for a long time.

The K9 officer was very distraught that he, as White policeman, had to shoot a Black man. But I assured him he had to do it to save his life and the life of his dog. This criminal was shooting too, so it had to be done. I was there to help these officers as well as to help their families. I also helped the victims of the families that were facing difficult times. I helped a number of times with the domestic disturbance calls as many times children were at the scene of the trauma. I helped whenever I could. It is really good for a police department to see the value of police chaplains.

So we left Indiana to move to Michigan. We're looking for a house to buy in the Muskegon area. It is Nancy's hometown. My relatives helped us in the search for a house. Jane and Mark spent a lot of time helping us. I saw a house between Muskegon and Ravenna that looked like a good match for our family. We put a bid on a house, and the owners accepted our offer. But when I saw a picture of the house that had accepted our offer, it was the *wrong* house! That is not the house I thought I was bidding on. We had stacks of reality papers, and I just bid on the *wrong* house. But in reality, it was just the house the Lord wanted us to have and the exact location where he wanted me to be.

There was a little one-room Baptist church right down the street from our home. It was a one-room schoolhouse and now was the home of this little church. It had been built in 1890. It was old! They had about twenty-five people in the church. We visited there, and when they found out I was an ordained Baptist minister, Jim French—the head deacon—let me do pulpit supply when the pastor needed me to fill in. This was about 2003, and I did pulpit supply there for the next two years.

In the meantime, I was working at a rescue mission in Grand Rapids on third shift. In the winter months, we had about 275 men a night housed at our mission, and about 30 of these men were mentally ill. And there were also about 60 to 80 women and children housed on the other half of the mission. I will come back and talk about the miracles God performed at the little Baptist Church, but first I want to share the many stories I have from working at the rescue mission.

Many of these 275 men were drunks, druggies, criminals, thieves, addicted to a host of evil sins, and sometimes violent. Our goal was to help them with their physical needs—such as food, shelter, clothes—and also to help them with their spiritual needs, such as salvation and deliverance from their addictions. I literally hated full moons because there were so many of them that acted crazy during a full moon, and especially at night on my third shift.

Terry was a schizophrenic. On full moons, he would get up about midnight, come down stairs, and say to me, "I hear voices. Did I ever tell you that I hear voices?"

I would say to him, "Yes, Terry, you have told me you hear voices. And do you know what the voices are saying to you? They are saying, 'Go upstairs and go to bed.'"

And he would say, "Okay," and he would go upstairs and go back to bed. About thirty minutes later, he would come downstairs and do the same thing all over again.

He would say again, "I hear voices. Did I ever tell you I hear voices?"

And I would repeat the same answer to him, and he would go back upstairs to bed. He would do this over and over until about 3:00 a.m., and then he would fall to sleep.

While Terry was doing that, Maurice would be in the upstairs bathroom, yelling at himself in the mirror. The other men would call me up on the intercom and say, "Maurice is at it again."

So I would go upstairs and have Maurice come down to the chapel. It was empty, and I would tell him he could yell in there. He would run around the room in circles, yelling, twirling for about three hours. He would finally go to sleep after he wore himself out. In the meantime, the local police department would bring a man in handcuffs that had been picked up for public intoxication. The police would ask me if the drunk could sleep off the night at our mission instead for filling up a jail cell downtown. I would tell them yes, and we would put the drink in our drunk tank room where other intoxicated men were being placed. About an hour later, two men came running out of the room.

They would be screaming, "That drunk just peed on us!" The drunk thought he was standing over a urinal and peed on the men. But before I could get him settled, he was now peeing in the public drinking fountain, thinking he was in the bathroom. Another man in the drunk tank room, we nicknamed him Lightbulb because his head was shaped like a lightbulb, was pounding his head against the drywall, trying to break the drywall. Another drunk who was violent was throwing stones at the front glass doors because we would not let him in because he was violent when he was drunk.

And another man who looked just like Kramer of the TV show *Seinfeld* was standing up in the bedroom, screaming as he pointed to a passed-out man of the floor, "He's a homosexual. He's a homosexual. He touched me."

The passed-out man on the floor was on a floor mat next to "Kramer" and had rolled over and accidentally touched the other man on a floor mat. So I had to bring "Kramer" downstairs too to settle down.

We worked well with the local police department. One night, about 2:00 a.m., two police officers stopped by and asked if they could look over our bed list to see if any of the men who were wanted were sleeping here. One problem, and I disagreed with the men's director over this, was he did not require any ID for the men to sleep there. So we had men check in with names like Jack Frost, Ronald McDonald, Charlie Brown, Ben Franklin, and other false names. This was so dangerous because we had murderers and rapists staying there at times under false names. Well, the officers recognized five names on the list as men who had outstanding warrants for illegal drugs.

So I said, "Okay, let's go up and get them." This room had about a hundred men in bunk beds, and all five men were in this room. When I got to the door, I went into the room, and they stopped at the door and did not come in.

I said, "Well, come on, let's go get them."

They said, "We are not going in the room."

I said, "Why not?"

And they said, "If we arrest one of them in that room, we will probably get jumped by the other men," and they probably would have been assaulted.

I said to them, "Well, you have the guns."

And they said again, "We are not going in there."

I said, "So do you want me to go in there with my pencil and say, 'Hey, you are under arrest'?"

They said, "No, but can you bring them out one at a time?"

I said, "Well, I will try."

I went to the first wanted man, shook his bed to wake him up, and said, "Hey, there is someone here to see you. You need to get up and come and see him. It's important."

He said to me, "Who is it?"

I said, "I don't know their names," and I didn't know because I didn't even look at their name tags.

So he got up, followed me out of the room, the police were behind the door, and they said, "Put your hands in the air."

They handcuffed him and took him to a waiting squad car downstairs. I went the second man, did the same exact scenario, and he was arrested and placed in a squad car. It went smoothly, one man at a time, until I had all five men out of the room—all five were arrested, and all five were taken to jail. But all the while I was taking these five men out one at a time, there was another man lying right by the door, and he was watching me very intently with his eyes. His eyes followed me as I walked in and walked out, walked in and walked out, etc.

The next morning, we would serve the men breakfast before sending them out for the day. Then they would come back each evening to get a supper and lodging for the night. At breakfast, this man who was watching me said, "Hey, Smith."

I said, "Yes."

He said, "Those five men all walked out with you last night." He paused. "And they didn't come back! Do you know why?"

I started laughing, and I said to him, "Yes, I know why, but I'm not telling you!"

He didn't ask twice; he must have figured out why. I did pay a personal price for instances like this. Twice, my car windows were broken out in revenge, and once, someone peed in my gas tank. When I tried to start the car the next morning, my car ran terrible. You would think with all the alcohol they drank it would be high-octane pee. But it sure wasn't. So I got to a gas station two blocks away and put premium gas in my tank and then it ran fine. I also bought a locking gas cap so that would not happen again. I drove three-hundred-dollar cars down there at night just for that reason so it wouldn't cost me a nice car.

I had people get mad at me when I was pastoring too. There are a number of reasons a person can get mad at the pastor. Sometimes it may be because the pastor is wrong, and sometimes it may be because a person is immature in their faith and they misunderstand the pastor. Sometimes it's just the devil getting someone stirred up over nothing. One millennial young woman got mad at the content of my sermon. It was all biblical but not politically correct.

And I would tell the congregation, "This sermon today will not be politically correct, but it will be biblically correct." Right in the middle of my message, she got up, stormed through the back doors of the church, and went home. When someone got mad at me, I would contact them, ask if I could sit down, and talk the matter over with them. So she let me talk with her. I explained the reason while I held to the position on that matter: that it was biblically based. And then I told her like I told so many people, "We can agree to disagree agreeably and still be friends." I always tried to have and show compassion to the other person.

Another time, a mother caused a big ruckus in our parking lot. We were having Vacation Bible School. And this mother (I'll call her Emma) had divorced her husband, and there was an ongoing custody dispute over their daughter. At this particular time, the ex-husband had custody of the child. But the mother came with her new boyfriend, and they were waiting in our parking lot in their car for the little girl to come out of the church.

Sure enough, when the child came out after the VBS was over, the mother raced over, snatched up the child in her arms, and jumped in the car with her boyfriend. Just at that moment, the real dad had showed up; he saw Emma grab the child and jump into the car. I ran over to the car myself to try to see what was going on. The dad came over and drew his arm and fist back to hit the boyfriend right through the driver's window. That's all we need, is a fistfight in the church parking lot with children and parents all watching.

I said to the dad, "Stop! Don't do that. I'll call the police."

So the boyfriend and Emma raced out of the parking lot with the child in their car. They easily could have run a child over in their haste to get away. This is a totally unacceptable situation.

I did call the police. The officer came out, heard the story, and had this advice to the dad. "This is a civil matter, and I can't go and take the child back. You will have to get this settled in court." I asked the office what I could do to prevent this from happening again. He suggested I call the county prosecutor, which I did the next day.

The prosecutor gave me some good advice. He said that even though the church is open to the public, it is technically privately owned land. It is in the hands of the trustees of the church. He said I literally could have an officer come next time and have her arrested for disturbing the peace.

This was going to be a hard-and-difficult phone call for me. I called Emma and told her what the prosecutor told me. And then I told her if she ever did that again, I would call the police and have her arrested. I further told her she is welcome to come there to a Sunday service in a peaceable manner but not to disturb the peace. She did not come back for about a year.

A year later, Emma came to church on Father's Day. Something had changed in her life. She had accepted Christ as her Savior, and she was a different person. She actually brought me a beautiful hanging basket of flowers to give me for Father's Day. Of course, I very graciously thanked her and told her I loved her. Jesus forgives us of all our sins, and we surely have to forgive people their offenses even if they don't ask for forgiveness. This heart that Jesus gave me was full of compassion, love, and forgiveness. Almost every time a person got mad at me in the church over something, we ended up being friends again, praise the Lord.

Humor in the Ministry

There was humor in my work at the mission. One night, as I was walking past the bathroom in the upstairs dormitory room, I heard someone saying, "Pull, pull!" I figured this was going to be interesting. I opened the door, and a man named Sid had a prosthetic leg from the knee down. He was sitting in a chair, and another man was pulling on the false leg; he was trying to get it off so Sid could take a shower. But the leg would not come off. He looked at me with such pitiful eyes and said, "Will you pull my leg off?"

I walked over to Sid and said, "How can I help you?"

He said, "Take ahold of my foot, turn the foot and leg ninety degrees, and then pull hard."

So I did that, and the leg popped right off. There was a stainless-steel rod sticking out of his kneecap that the leg would fasten to keep the leg in place. I pulled his leg and then handed it to him so he could take a shower.

This instance reminds me of another story. I would tell this story to the churches that I pastored. Years ago, I was able to go on a missionary trip to India. We were going to take Bibles and other items to a village located deep in the jungles of India. So we flew by plane to New Delhi. We then traveled by jeep as far as the roads would take us. Then we went down Banjar River by canoes until we came to the trail that would lead us to this remote village in the jungle. Our guide warned us to be very careful of spiders, snakes, and other creatures that could harm us in the brush. He said one particular problem was, the boa constrictors would lay on a tree limb over the trails and drop down on its victim and squeeze them to death.

As we started down the trail, it was quite narrow. Brush was very close to us on both sides, and we could see large spider webs and small bugs running across the trail. I was trying to be very careful to not touch anything along the brushy trail. I was the last one in the party of five people as we walked along the trail. I went under a large tree limb and ducked a little bit to get under it.

All of a sudden, I heard a loud thud behind me. A large boa constrictor had been lying on that tree limb and had waited for everyone else to pass and decided I would be its next meal. It was a huge snake! Its head was about eight inches across, and its body was about a foot thick. It stared slithering toward me. Its tongue was a foot long, and it was sticking its tongue in and out to pick up my scent.

As it started coming at me, I took off running down that trail! But the snake was slithering very quickly toward me. That snake was fast, and it was gaining on me! I came to another tree with a low-hanging branch, and I grabbed it and pulled myself up off the trail. The snake came in quickly; its tongue poking in and out to find me. It got right to the spot where I jumped up in the tree and stopped! Its head was moving back and forth to find me. It came to the bottom of the tree and started slithering up the tree! It must have sensed me somehow. So quickly I climbed up higher in the tree.

The snake was coiling around the trunk, and with each turn around the tree, it was coming up higher to get me. I went as high in the tree as I could, and I could not get any higher. The snake came up to my foot, and I tried kicking it back. He took its massive head and mouth and latched onto my foot! And then he started pulling and pulling and pulling my leg, just like I'm pulling your leg! Did I get you? I had more fun telling that story to children, teens, and adults, and most of the time, I did pull their leg. A little humor is good for the soul.

Seriously, there were some laughable times at the mission. One night, a large Black man, about six feet and three inches, had passed out on the toilet inside one of the stalls in the upstairs bathroom. He was so tall he fell forward, still sitting on the toilet, and his body was leaning against the stall door so I could not get the door open. I crawled under the stall and was standing next to him. He was as tall sitting on the toilet as I was tall standing next to him. He was big! I grabbed both of his shoulders and pulled him back off the door.

Suddenly he woke up and he yelled at me, "What are you doing in here?"

My life flashed before me; I knew I was about to get beaten to death by a big Black man inside a bathroom stall!

So I said very quickly, "You passed out here in the stall. I'm trying to help you."

He realized I was trying to help him, and he said, "Okay."

I got the door opened and had him laid on the floor until the ambulance arrived. There were a number of times men would pass out at the mission. Sometimes they were drunk, sometimes they had low sugar, and sometimes they had epilepsy or some other medical condition. The ambulance came and took him to the hospital. He turned out to be okay.

We had a little Chinese man who went by the English name of Eddie. I don't know what his Chinese name was, but he went by the name Eddie. He was barley five feet tall and weighed about ninety pounds. He was short and about one brick short of a full load. He would take his hands and fingers and make them in the shape of a pistol with his index fingers, pointing straight out, and he would say, "I killed JFK (President John F. Kennedy), and I kill you too!" But we all knew he was harmless, just a little crazy.

One winter night, I saw Eddie did not have a coat. I gave him a nice winter coat. The next night, he came in without a coat again. I figured someone stole it from him because he was so small. The next night, he came into the mission again without a coat. So I gave him another one. I did this four nights in a row. One of the other homeless men came up to me and said, "Do you know what Eddie is doing with those coats you gave him?"

I said, "What is Eddie doing with those coats?"

He said, "Eddie is selling each coat for a bottle of wine." Now that is what you call a true alcoholic.

So the next day, as I was giving Eddie his fifth coat, I said to him, "Eddie, I heard what you did with those four coats. You sold them for a cheap bottle of wine. Eddie, listen to me, this is the last coat I'm going to give you. If you sell this coat, I will not give you another one, and I will send you out for the day in your T-shirt. I'm not letting you get booze from me anymore."

The next day, Eddie came into the mission without a coat. He had sold it for a bottle of wine. We kept him overnight, and I did send him out into the cold in his T-shirt the next day. He was going to have to use someone else to get his cheap booze. The last I heard of Eddie, he went up to police officer, made his hands and fingers to look like a pistol, and said to the cop, "I kill JFK, and I kill you too." He was taken to a mental hospital, and I haven't heard from him since.

I gave a pair of tennis shoes to a man named Marvin. He was one brick short of a full load too. About 1:00 a.m., I saw Marvin sitting in a parking lot across from the mission. He was sitting Indian style and holding his hands over a small fire. So I went over to see him. He was holding his hands over his burning tennis shoes that I had given him. I said, "Marvin, what are you doing?"

He said, "I'm warming my hands."

I said, "Marvin, come into the mission, and I'll give you another pair of shoes." I pushed the burning shoes to the curb to finish burning out and took Marvin into the mission to sleep that night. Someone drove by and saw the shoes on fire and called the fire department. They came out with a great big truck and extinguished those burning shoes. Your tax dollars were hard at work!

Another man named John was staying at our mission. At breakfast, we had a good meal for the men. We had eggs, pancakes, sausage, coffee, juice, and cereal. When John went through the food line the first time, he was served all the good hot food. When he went through the line for seconds, we were out of sausage. So he goes through the line, he walks over to me with his tray without sausage, he sticks the tray under my nose, and he said to me, "Thanks for nothing." What an ingrate.

So I said to him, "For the next two days, you will not be allowed to eat here. I'm going to bar you for two days from coming here, and maybe when you come back, you will appreciate the food you get."

I did bar him for two days. And I didn't know he had been barred from the other missions in town because of his bad behavior, so he had no place to stay. He made a big placard, which covered the front of his chest. He wrote on it, "I'm homeless because of Dan Smith." And he walked back and forth for two days in front of our mission wearing that stupid sign. No, he wasn't homeless because of Dan Smith.

Someone said to me, "What did you do to John?"

I said, "Nothing, he did it to himself." He was homeless because he had acted like a fool in every mission where he had stayed. When he did come back, he never complained to me about the food again!

Another winter night, a young man came into the mission about midnight. He didn't have on any shoes or socks, and he just had brown jersey gloves over the toes on both of his feet. The gloves were soaked from the wet snow, and his feet were really red. He was wearing a placard on both sides of his body. The front said, "I will not wear shoes until you listen to me." The back said, "Reward for lost backpack, $1.00." Yeah right, someone was going to return it for a dollar.

Well, I tried to offer him shoes and socks, and he would not take them until I listened to him. Now I have a full mission of people, and I don't have time to listen to this nut, but I had mercy on him. I told him I would listen to him. He took out a big scroll, unrolled it like Benjamin Franklin would have done, and started reading. It was the rantings of a nut! So after I listened to all his rantings, he put on the shoes and socks. Later that year, this man was arrested for being a pyromaniac. He had torched ten garages before he was arrested. But God was using all these people to help me get more patience. To be a pastor, you must have tremendous patience. And God was accomplishing that in me.

We had a number of homosexuals and transgender men stay at our mission. One night, I got a call from another mission that was nearby. They said they had a problem and needed my help. I asked what the problem was, and they said they had a man who was now a woman and they didn't keep women at their mission and asked if I would take him/her. So I said, yes, I would.

When he came in the door, he really was made into a woman. He had all the surgeries to make him look like a woman, with boobs and female hormones. He was quite young too.

So I said to him, "Okay, come sign our bed list, and I'll give you a bed for the night."

He said to me, "I'm sleeping on the woman's side."

I said, "No, you are not!"

He said to me, "Why not?"

And I said to him, "You were born a man, and you are sleeping on the men's side." Those women over there didn't want a mixed-up man sleeping near them or their children.

He said to me, "If you don't let me sleep on the women's side, I will sue you."

I said, "You go right ahead and sue me. The answer is no, you are sleeping on the men's side."

He said to me, "Who is your boss?"

I said, "God is my boss, and you are sleeping on the men's side."

He said again, "I will sue you."

And I told him again, "You go right ahead and sue me. This organization does not take public funds. This is our house with our rules, and if you stay here, you are going to abide by our rules." I was not backing down.

So he came for three nights in a row. He threatened me again with a lawsuit, and I gave him the same answer every time, "You are sleeping on the men's side." He finally quit coming, and I never saw him/her again.

We had other transgender men come into the mission; I can truly tell you, their thinking was really mixed up. Evangelist Bob Jones used to say, "Give God your heart and he will comb all the kinks out of your head." These poor men sure needed the Lord. We obviously believe in conversion therapy. God is able and willing to spiritually fix any human being who will turn their heart and mind over to him.

We had a lot of thieves that stayed at the mission. One night, a Hispanic man came to me and said someone had stolen his phone. I asked him if the phone was turned on, and he said, "Yes, it is."

I said to him, "Let's go upstairs to the men's dormitory, and I'll dial your phone number and see who has your phone."

These homeless people were not short on cellphones. They were given free Obama phones by the government, and some men had three or four of these free phones because they had used three or four different names to sign up for the free phones. Your tax dollars hard at work. I stopped at the doorway where the men were sleeping in their bunks, and I dialed his phone number. Sure enough, the man in bed 36 had the Hispanic man's phone; it was ringing.

I went over to bed 36, and the phone was ringing under the covers; and the man in bed was faking like he was asleep and didn't hear the phone.

I said to him, "Come on, man, I know you got his phone."

The man didn't open his eyes or even move, and the phone was still ringing under his covers. So I grabbed the blanket and pulled it down, and the phone was ringing inside this man's boxers! He had shoved it inside his underwear. So now he opens his eyes and says, "Who put that phone if my underwear?"

I said to him, "Oh sure, you mean to tell me someone came over to your bed and shoved this phone down into your underwear, and you didn't know it?"

He didn't answer, so I said to him, "Give this Hispanic man his phone back."

So he reached down into his boxers, pulled the phone out, and gave it to its owner. Then the Hispanic man said to me, "Where is the charger?"

I said to the thief in bed 36, "Where is his charger?" He had that stuffed down into his boxers too! Yuck!

I said to the thief, "Come downstairs for the rest of the night. I'm not leaving a thief up here in the dorm room."

He came downstairs, and I don't ever remember seeing that man come in again.

We had a young man named Robert that worked in our auto donation program. He was an addict, and we working to get his life back together. He would wash and detail all the cars that we repaired before we put them up for sale on the front lot.

One day, we had an Astro van that had been donated to the mission. It had been sitting in tall grass out in the snow for who knows how long. It was pushed into the garage and into a hoist area to be lifted up for inspection to see what all had to be done to make it drivable again. I opened the hood, and there were a couple of mice nests under the hood. Then I found a shed snakeskin inside the radiator area. A snake had gone up into the van to get the mice. Robert was walking by just as I found that snakeskin. I held it, and it was about two feet long. And I said, "Robert, look what I found."

He said, "You be thinking there be snakes still alive in that van?"

I said, "When the van thaws out, we'll find out."

He yelled, "I ain't cleaning that van. I ain't cleaning that van!"

So later in the day, I found another shed snakeskin inside of the van. I held it up just like the other one and said, "Robert…" and wiggled the skin.

He yelled again, "I ain't cleaning that van!"

I found a total of five mice nests in that van.

When the van was finished and driven over to the wash bay for him to be cleaned, Robert would never go all the way into the van. He would put one foot in the van and have the other foot on the concrete floor, ready to run in an instant!

The Serious Side of the Ministry

I was working this job and was only getting $7.50 an hour. I sure wasn't there for the pay. If you ever thought you had bad working conditions, don't come complaining to me. I had my hands in human blood so many times working at the mission. Men would stumble in all beat up and bloody, and I would reach out to stop them from falling down and get blood all over my hands. We had men whose stomachs ruptured from drinking alcohol and would have blood all over them and the floor, and we would assist them and then call for an ambulance. Men had bloody noses and other reasons why they got blood on a door handle or railing on the stairs. I had a bottle of bleach water on hand, and with the bleach and the Lord helping me, I never got AIDS or hepatitis, or any other disease.

There was a man coming to the mission whose name was John. He was a terrible alcoholic. He drank and drank and drank. He stopped eating most of the time and was existing on a liquid diet of alcohol. The alcohol would run right through him, and he had liquid diarrhea. He crapped his pants, and the diarrhea ran down both of his legs and into his shoes. His shoes were literally filled with human waste, and he smelled terrible. He stumbled into the mission. I helped him get to the bathroom, and he ended up passing out on sitting on the toilet. I had a coworker help me, and we picked him up, carried him to our drunk tank room, and got some fresh clothes for him.

He woke up. I said to him, "John, here are some clean clothes, and there is a shower right over there where you can get cleaned up."

He said, "I'm not taking a shower." The diarrhea that had run down his legs and was literally caked between his toes on both feet. He was a mess.

I said, "John, you have crap all over you, and you need to take a shower."

He said no, and he put those clean clothes on right over his messy, stinky body. He put those nasty crap-filled shoes right back on his feet. When he stood up to leave, I said to him, "John, you are going to die. You have to stop drinking." He did not answer me, and he stumbled out the door. Two days later, John was found dead in a back alley. He had literally drank himself to death.

Another man named Ron was in his mid-thirties. He was a former vet and had fallen on hard times because of his PTSD and was staying at the mission. He came downstairs one morning, about two o'clock, and wanted to talk with me. We chatted for a while, and then I asked him questions to see if he was a born-again Christian. We talked for about one hour. He was not saved, but said he would think about our discussion. The next evening, they found him facedown in the snow. He wasn't breathing, and there wasn't any pulse. So his body was taken to the morgue. When his body started warming up, he started twitching his toes. He came back to life after he thawed out, but because his brain was without oxygen for who knows how long, his brain functioning was that of a child. He spent the rest of his days in a nursing home.

Another man named Steve came to our mission. He was such an alcoholic and was going through withdrawals that he could not hold a glass or a spoon. He was shaking so bad we had to feed him by hand. He had been at the Woodstock rock concert in the '60s and had been a drinker for decades. We had to feed him by hand for a few days so when he quit shaking so badly, he could feed himself. He went through our rehab program and quit drinking. He got a new job, a car, and was building up his bank account. He had been at our mission about one year. He went back home to some kind of graduation party, and alcohol was being served. Steve took one drink, and he went back into relapse. A few months later, I heard Steve was dead. He drank himself to death.

Sometimes a spiritual battle takes place with a pastor or a deacon board. It shouldn't be that way, but if a spiritual leader is being carnal in the flesh, these encounters do happen.

Once a month, we would give a free auto from our auto donation program to a needy family. We gave discounts to pastors who needed a car. One day, a pastor came to our shop. He had his own mechanic with him. He had purchased a car from us, at a discount of course. His teenage son was driving the car, and the engine spun a bearing. To spin a bearing in an engine requires high RPMs above five thousand, even closer to seven thousand, which will damage any normal engine. There had just been a big snowstorm, and we got many inches of snow. I figured his teenage son got stuck in the snow, and he had raced the engine to high RPMs to get unstuck and spun the bearing, which ruined the engine.

This pastor was complaining to Bill, our master mechanic, that we had sold him a bad car. He had his own mechanic with him, and he was backing up the pastor's story. I figured he was a member of the pastor's church. He, too, said we sold the pastor a bad car. When the suggestion was made that maybe it was the way the pastor's son had been driving, the pastor's response was, "My son is a good driver and drives like a grandmother." Oh brother, yeah, like maybe the little old lady from Pasadena. I could not believe the pastor could be so naive about his son. I wasn't impressed with the pastor's mechanic that he would believe such a story too.

The pastor wasn't asking for another free car; he was demanding we give him a free car. I was really upset that he was being so demanding. I wanted so bad to have a pastor-to-pastor talk with him. The next morning, I got my chance to do so.

I arrived early before the shop was unlocked. This pastor was also standing by the door, waiting to get inside to talk to Bill again. I thought to myself, *Thank you, Lord, I'm going to talk to this pastor*.

I said to him, "Good morning. I am a mechanic at this shop, and I also am a pastor at church myself. You sure are making yourself look bad. Your son spun that bearing by driving too hard, and you are making yourself look bad as a pastor by demanding that you get another free car. You need to stop being so unreasonable about all of this."

By the expression on his face, I knew he was mad at me. He said he would come back later and walked away. He knew I was right in what I told him, but he continued to be carnal anyway. I caught Ben when he came into the office. I told him what had happened, and I was sure that "man of God" was going to complain about me. Sure enough, that is exactly what he did! So after he talked to Ben, Ben came to see me.

He said, "Well, he talked to me, all right, and he did not like what you told him." Then Ben said to me, "I'm so glad you told him what you did. I wanted to tell him that, but I'm not a pastor."

I asked Ben, "What did you and Bill decide?"

He said, "We are going to show grace and give him another car." They gave him a car, and I never saw that pastor come back again. Doesn't the Bible say a wise man listens to rebuke? Over the years, I have seen so many pastors, deacons, and so-called spiritual leaders in the church cause so much harm by being carnal. I sure wouldn't want to be a member of his church.

One day, and an older White man and a very short Black man were walking up to our shop. I greeted them at the garage door. The older man said, "I met this man on the street, and he was hungry. So I bought him breakfast. And he is really sick. Can you give him some money to help him?"

I knew this little man. He was one of our mental cases that stayed at the mission every night. I was sure he had eaten breakfast already at the mission that morning and was making a sucker out of the older man. The older man had a good heart but not the brains to realize he was being suckered.

So I said to the short man, "I know you. You stay at the mission, and you already had breakfast at the mission first thing this morning."

And the short man shook his head yes. The older man's mouth started to drop open as he was now realizing what was going on here.

Then I said to the short man, "And I know that if we give you some money, you are going to go and buy some booze."

And he shook his head yes and said, "Yup, that's what I'll do." Now the older man's mouth had fully dropped open. And then I said to the short man, "And if you are really sick, I'll call an ambulance right now." St. Mary's hospital was good about giving medical help to the homeless people.

And he said to me. "No, no, that's okay. I don't need an 'amblance.' I'll be just fine." And he walked away. This poor older man learned a good lesson that day. Almost all the panhandlers you see out on street corners only want cash so they can buy drugs or alcohol, and you are not helping them by giving them money. You are only making things worse. There are literally five places in Grand Rapids where a homeless man can get five hot meals a day.

When President Gerald Ford died, he was going to be buried in a grassy plot located right in front of the Gerald R. Ford Museum in Grand Rapids, Michigan. People lined up by the hundreds to stand along the street to see the presidential procession drive by. Nancy and I lined up on the street so we could see the hearse. Because this was a former President, the air space had been closed over that area, and there were military helicopters hovering right above the street. We could also see a sniper mounted and stationed up on top of one of the tallest buildings downtown.

As we were waiting for the hearse to drive by, I saw a man with a gallon of gas can walking along the route of people and saying, "My car is out of gas. Can you give me some money for gas?"

When he got up to where I was standing, I said to him, "You don't recognize me, but I work at the mission. And I've seen you stay there, and you don't even own a car!"

He looked at me with a shocked look on his face, and then I said, "Get you and your gas can out of here, and stop begging for money." He walked past me and a little further down the line; he was doing the same thing all over again,

"My car is out of gas. Can you give me some money to buy gas?" Don't give money to the men on the street.

There was another homeless man named Lightbulb because his head and neck were shaped like a lightbulb. Nancy and I were standing in another line in Grand Rapids, Michigan, to see Steve Smith. He was that main actor of that very funny TV show called *The Red Green Show*. He was going to be performing that afternoon at the Grand Rapids Civic Theatre. I looked down the line of people, and here was Lightbulb begging for money. He was already tipsy and didn't recognize me. He held out his hand and asked me for some money. When Lightbulb got drunk, he got violent. He was the same man I told about who would try to drive his head through the drywall in the mission drunk tank room.

So I said to him, "You don't recognize me, Donald, but I work at the mission. And if I give you some money, you will just go and get drunk." I said it loud enough so others standing by would not give him some money too. But there was a bleeding-heart liberal there by me, and she reached down into her purse and put a wad of money into his hand! That was the worst thing she could have done, and he literally took off running to get to the liquor store to buy booze. I was really disgusted. I figured because of this woman's lack of good sense, now I would have to deal with Lightbulb that evening. Don't give money to street people!

One of the women who had come to our mission was named Sally. I won't use her real name because she had an unusual name, and if I give it, some people will recognize who she is; and I don't want to speak bad of her, but I do want to tell her story so it might keep someone from doing what she had done.

Sally was a drunk and drug addict. She signed up for our in-house treatment program and was successful. She broke her habits, and now she was hired to work third shift with me. And she was supervising on the women's side of the building. She was really doing a great job. One day she did not come to work, then another day, and soon she was not coming in at all. I inquired about her, and they said she had relapsed.

About one year later, she showed back up to the mission. She was terribly thin. She had damaged her liver. She was a Black woman, but I have never seen a Black woman look so yellow. Her eyes were yellow, her skin and palms were yellow. She was dying. It wasn't too long after that and I heard she had died. If I can just keep one teenager to make a decision to never drink alcohol, then this book and these stories are worth all time it has taken to write this all down.

> Wine is a mocker, and strong drink is ragging, and whoever is deceived thereby is not wise.
> (Proverbs 20:1)

Some people say it's okay to drink alcohol because there is wine in the Bible. What they don't realize is that many times the word *wine* is used, it is unfermented grape juice. Here is what God clearly says about drinking alcohol.

> Who has woe? Who has sorrows? Who has contentions? Who has babblings? Who has wounds without cause? Who has redness of the eyes? They that tarry long at the wine, they that go to seek [fermented alcohol]. Look not upon the wine when it [ferments], when it giveth it's color in the cup; when it is [churning with fermentation]. Your eyes will behold strange women, and your heart will utter perverse things. Yes, you will be [in a stumbling stupor], you will say they have beaten me, and I was not sick, they have beaten me, and I felt it not; when I awake? I will [crave] it again. (Proverbs 23:29–35)

None of these men or women said to themselves when they were teens that they would grow up and become an alcoholic or living on the street or under bridges. None of them said to themselves when they were young that they would grow up, crap their pants, end up in a nursing home, or die from alcohol in a back alley. Most people think it will not happen to them.

I substitute in three Christian schools here in Florida. I have told these stories in all three schools to the middle and high school teens. My hope is that they will make a decision to never drink alcohol or take illegal drugs. I believe these stories will have an impact on some teens. So whenever I get a chance to tell these stories to middle school or high school students, I do so.

Building the Kingdom of God

Part 2

While I was working at the rescue mission, I would drive right by the little Baptist church that was one mile from my home. I am purposely not giving the name of this church, nor am I going to mention any names of the men in the leadership of that church who took over after I left. I don't want to slander the name of the church, nor any of the men who did a terrible job of ruining the church after I left.

I had been doing pulpit supply for them about two years now. As I drove home this one particular day, it was really impressed on my home to become the pastor of that church. I said to the Lord, "If that pastor ever leaves that church, I would like to be the pastor of that church."

The next Sunday, the pastor resigned, and all that were left were eight people. The church was run-down, smelly, and it looked like it was ready to close. My dear friend Jim French, who was the elder of the church, called me and asked me if I would become the pastor of that church. He said they would take a vote the next Sunday and let me know.

There are two things that changed my life forever. The first one was when I got saved. The second one happened with this church. Jim called me up the next Sunday and told me the church voted for me to be the pastor; would I accept? When I said yes over the phone, God did something supernatural to me. I felt him figuratively open up my chest and put a brand-new heart into my chest.

It was a true pastor's heart, full of love, compassion, grace, kindness, mercy, patience, and a sacrificial love for his flock. It changed me forever! I felt it was my job to not only teach these dear people, but also to show the love of Jesus as it flowed from his heart through my heart to the people. The pay was only fifty dollars a week to be the pastor, but it wasn't about the money. It was about serving the Lord.

A dear friend and saint named Ann Ruse came to visit. She said she could see that I had a true pastor's heart, and she would know because her son was also a pastor in Indiana. She joined our church and was a vital part of the church all the way through to the New Building program.

Nancy and I rolled up our sleeves and went to work to build up this church for the Lord. First, we replaced the broken front door of the church. Then we found black mold in the basement, and we bleached every wall and painted them with mildew-resistant paint. We put a cute white picket fence around the church to match the cute white building. I had a man build a new bell steeple to match what the original building had looked like. Then I started loving those people and preaching my heart out. Jesus said he would build his church, and I was trusting him to do just that. The first Sunday I was there, a man that was known for being cantankerous walked up to my face.

Jim Quinn said, "I don't like Republicans. I don't like Christian schools [he heard that I was a substitute teacher for area Christian schools], and I don't know if I like you."

I was looking him right in the eyes, and that pastor's heart that God gave me just pumped out a boatload of love, and I said to him, "Jim, I don't care what you say. I will always love you."

He became my friend for life. I could ask him to do anything for that church; he was a handyman, and he would always do it. When he had a serious motorcycle accident and he was lying in the road, he called me before he even called an ambulance and wanted me there—which, of course, I did.

One day, Jim was cutting wood on a table saw, and he cut his three fingers right in half down the center of his fingers, about one inch down on each finger. Instead of calling an ambulance, he called me and asked me to rush to his house. When I got there, blood was splattered everywhere. There was blood sprayed all over the white ceiling of that shed, on the table saw—blood splattered all over. He was holding his fingers with his other hand.

I said, "Jim, I'll drive you to the hospital."

He said, "I'm not going."

I said, "Jim, you have to get those fingers sewed up and get a tetanus shot."

He said, "No, I'm not going."

So I said to him, "What do you want me to do?"

He said, "I want you to tape my fingers back together."

I said, "Okay."

So I took black electrical tape and taped all three of his fingers back together again so the gap that ran down the middle of all three of his fingers would be closed. With his fingers healed, the two halves of each finger grew back together. He didn't get tetanus, but he also lost the feeling at the end of each of those fingers, He recently passed away from a heart attack. I miss him so much, but I'll see him again in heaven.

Well, my second Sunday of being the pastor at the church God sent a family of six to visit us. Tom and Susan had four children, so Nancy took them downstairs; and that was the start of our new junior church program. They came every week. We started with eight people, and in two weeks, we almost doubled. But it was a sign from God that he was going to build this church up, and it was going to be successful.

Of the eight people I started the church with, two of them were deacons. Jim French was the elder, and Walt Soderstrom was the treasurer. They both had been at that church for decades and had keep it going—barely—but kept it going since the 1950s. Walt said to me that he liked to go calling to people's homes and invite them to church. I love doing home visitations. So Walt and I worked so that we would visit every home within two square miles of the church. It took about six years to do so, and Walt was so faithful we went calling every week. And it worked! People started coming, and coming, and coming—praise the Lord.

Walt and I visited a very poor family that lived in the church neighborhood. It was a very dirty, smelly home; the stench of cat pee rolled out the front door as we stood there talking to the occupants. I'm not going to give their real names, and this would hurt their feelings. I will just say Jack and Jill. They both had mental deficiencies, and the woman much more so. They weren't married yet, but they were coming to my little church.

When they walked in, you literally could not sit next to them because their clothes were so bad. Nancy bought clothes from the mission store, where she was the manager, and we gave them fresh clothes. They decided to get married and asked me to perform the wedding ceremony, which I did. Jill did not have a wedding dress. It just so happened a store donated some leftover wedding dresses to her store, and we got a dress for Jill that fit her just right.

At the day of the wedding, Jack showed up with some new clothes we gave him. But he had wadded them up and never ironed them. He came in the church for the wedding, his clothes were wrinkled from top to bottom, and he asked me, "How do I look?"

It would break his heart if I told him something discouraging on his wedding day. And for him, even if the clothes were wrinkled, it was a miracle they were clean.

I said to him, "You look just fine," and for him that was as fine as it was ever going to get. I continued to minister to that family for many years before they moved on.

One Sunday, I was preaching to the people about loving the unlovely. I talked about punk rockers, homosexuals, lesbians, teens with pink or spiked hair, and even a filthy bum that might walk through our church doors. I said we are to love people no matter what they looked like. As soon as I said that, our back doors opened up, and here stood a tall thin man, with filthy clothes on, and his hair was all messy, and he appeared very poor;

He said, "Oh, I thought this was the place they were giving out free food today."

I said to him, "We can help you with that. Would you like to stay for the service?"

He said, "Where can I sit?"

And immediately I saw four or five of my people slide over and say, "You can sit next to me." And he did sit down. I was so proud of my people! God sent this man at exactly the time I said to love someone who may be filthy and poor, and my people responded with the love of Jesus!

When Walt and I visited his home, he literally had aluminum foil over all his windows. He didn't want radiation from the sun to come into his house. When he let us in, his couch was supposed to be brown, but the seat and arms of the couch were black with dirt. It was obvious he had mental problems. But wouldn't Jesus show love to him? And we did too.

Walt and I visited a home that was on my street to ask the family to come visit our church. I did not know the man was a Jehovah's Witness. He says he kicked me off his property. I don't remember that, but I try to just remember the good in people, not the bad.

So one night, about ten o'clock, I got a phone call. A man said he was sitting in my church parking lot. He got my phone number off the church sign, said he was thinking about suicide, and asked if I would come talk to him. Absolutely, I would always talk to someone like him. I did not know it was this Jehovah's Witness who had kicked me off his property, and he did not know it was me whom he had just called.

So when I drove up and got out of the car, he recognized me, but I did not remember him. So we talked quite awhile. Archie could see my heart that I truly cared about him. He started coming to my church. This was a miracle in itself that he would attend a Baptist church, but he had seen enough at the Kingdom Hall to turn him off to that religion. I was very patient with him, and he did not need or want any pressure like the Jehovah's Witnesses do to others. I told him I would not pressure him but asked him to come and just listen, and talk to me when he was ready.

We became personal friends right away. I really liked this guy. He came for maybe about one and a half years, and he understood the truth, realized he had been mistaught by the Kingdom Hall, and trusted Jesus as his Savior. That man now knows his doctrine very well, and he is really good at debating others' false views.

More importantly, we are lifelong friends. Archie grew spiritually, and he genuinely changed. One day, his neighbor plugged up a drainage tube that allowed water to flow away from Archie's house. As a result of it being plugged, Archie's basement had over a foot of water in it. So he confronted the neighbor, and the neighbor was being hard to reason with and he challenged Archie to do something about it. Archie told him, "Well, before I became a Christian, I would have beat you up, but now that I'm a Christian, I think I'll just baptize you in this water." I was really proud of Archie's answer. The neighbor did unplug that drain tube.

He met a girl online from the Philippines name Marjorie. She came to the United States for six weeks to see him. She was a Roman Catholic and came to my church every Sunday for six weeks. On the last Sunday, she asked to talk with me. I explained what it meant to really trust Jesus as her Savior, prayed with her right there in the church, and she really understood what it means to be born-again. They eventually got married and now have a precious son named Isaac.

Archie is the strongest man I have ever met. He was an avid weight lifter and still does weight lifting. One day, a poor inner-city woman who was attending my church got evicted from her home. She was given twenty-four hours to get her stuff out of the house. So I asked Archie and a couple of men to help me. Ranell had a refrigerator in her basement. She didn't even have time to empty it out. We loaded it on the two-wheel cart and tried to get it up some rickety wooden stairs. Suddenly, under the weight of the refrigerator, the cart wheel broke. Archie said, "Get out of the way." He wrapped his arms around that full refrigerator and literally carried it up the stairs by himself. I truly met a modern-day Samson. He would split his wood with a twenty-pound splitting maul. That man could really hurt someone. When he went to the Philippines to see his future wife, he was being kidnapped by three men. They picked the wrong guy to kidnap!

He was telling me the story, and I said, "Well, how did it all end up?"

He said, "Well, I have a broken watch, and they have three broken noses!"

Yeah, he gave them just what they deserved.

There was another young teenage boy that lived on the street of our church. His name is Casey. He would ride his bike down to church every Sunday. He accepted Christ as his Savior while attending my church as was in our youth group throughout his teen years. On rainy days, I would drive him and his bike home in the van that the mission had given me. He has a lot of special needs. He was in an abusive home, was put in foster care, was adopted, and then was unadopted. He has a lot of emotional issues and learning disabilities, but he is quite normal when talking with him. So he finished high school, and he had been my friend even after I retired from the church.

This summer, I have signed him up for driver's ed. I paid the course for him; I will drive him every day, let him learn to practice drive with my vehicle, and help him get his license. I told the driving school that he has learning disabilities. They said they would have him take the written test first by himself, and if he didn't do well, I would sit with him and orally read and help him grasp the questions. This literally means loving my neighbor and going the extra mile!

Casey's foster parents never got things worked out for him to take driver's ed, so he does not have a driver's license.

One day, a family came to visit, and I told a story about a sacrifice I made for my wife, Nancy. I was preaching from the verse Ephesians 5:25, where "husbands are to love their wives like Christ loved and died for the church." We were living in Goshen, Indiana, and I was teaching full time in a Christian school. Our daughter, Anissa, was about eight years old; our adopted son, Kenny, was about one year old; and Nancy had a miscarriage. She got pregnant right away, and she was having bleeding issues and was going to lose this baby too. The doctor said the only way she could save this baby was to stay in bed for the next six weeks; get to the fourth month of her pregnancy, and the baby might make it. So I'm now the cook, babysitter, dishwasher, Laundromat, etc. But the worst part was for her was to lie in bed for six weeks all-day long.

I didn't have much money teaching at a Christian school, but I had a really nice expensive shotgun. It was a Remington 1100 twelve-gauge shotgun with a walnut stock and a DuPont finish that was very shiny, and it was an automatic shotgun. I sold my best shotgun to help my wife. I got three hundred dollars for the gun. I bought a brand-new VCR, which had just come out, and a bunch of VHS tapes so she could stay in bed and watch all kinds of movies for six weeks. Well, it worked; she stayed in bed, and the baby was born. And that was our last child, Kevin.

So I told that story in church while that new family that was visiting. About two weeks later, this husband pulled up in my driveway in his car. He knocked on my door and asked me to come to his car. He opened the trunk, and there was a brand-new Remington 1100 twelve-gauge automatic shotgun in his trunk. He said he was so moved by my story he went out and bought me this gun. And this gun was better that the one I sold; this one had real gold inlaid into the gun receiver. God gave me back better than I gave away. And I was so thankful for the kindness of this man!

The church was growing. Our little building was packed at seventy people. We filled it up every Sunday. The parking lot was so small we asked Erma, one of our members that lived across the street from the church, if we could park the extra cars in her yard, and she said yes. Now when the neighborhood started seeing the overflow of people, then more people came. We had started junior church—Anissa, Dawn, Elaine, Bonnie, and Tanya taught the children. Nancy ran the nursery. Now we needed a youth group, so we started that too. And my son Kevin; his wife, Kristen; and Kim ran the youth group.

We had to start a second service to hold all the new people. We had about seventy in both services. The Lord continued to bless. Catholics, Jehovah's Witnesses, and many other people came and got saved at our church. And I loved them all with this pastor's heart. I started a little motto for our church, "A small country church with a big heart."

Offerings increased, and we were starting to save up to build a new church. That old building was so small; the nursery was also our coatroom and our sound room. It had a full basement and a small kitchen at one end. I added two new deacons to the deacon board. Nancy ran the nursery, junior church, women's Bible study, VBS, and all the other special programs and banquets.

The church continued to grow, and the people increased my pay with the growth. It still wasn't enough to go full time, but I was making $250 a week now. But I still had to work at the mission. This was so much stress; I was working at the mission on third shift full time, and I was pastoring full time too. It was wearing me out. I'll tell more about this later.

*****

Jim French, the elder of the board, was a retired cop with a big sense of humor. We teased each other a lot from the pulpit, and he always got the last word because I let him close the service in prayer while I made my way to the doors of the foyer so I could greet everyone as they left.

One day, Jim told a cop story. Back in his day, when he was a cop, the police officers did not carry their guns home. They checked them in and out of their shift. So Jim would carry a banana in his gun holster on his way to check in for his shift. One day, on the way in to his shift, there was an armed robbery in progress. He heard it on the radio, and it was right near him. So he drove over their really fast, pulled up to the store, reached for his gun, and all he had was a banana!

So the following Sunday, I got a big banana; and with a black marker, I wrote, "Dole 38 Special" on the side of the banana. I hid it under the pulpit until the church service started. When it came time for announcements, I said, "Jim, you remember that story you told last week about rushing to a robbery with a banana?"

He started laughing and said, "Yes."

I said, "Well, now I have a special banana for you to carry in your gun holster." And I pulled out the banana, called him up front, and gave him the Dole 38 Special. He said he kept that banana for two years in his freezer until it turned black. Jim was a very gifted elder. He backed me no matter what. When I would ask the board to go forward with a project, he would question whether he thought we could do it and when I presented the way we would work to get it done, he always supported me. He kept saying, "I want to live long enough to be in that new church."

The property right across the street went up for sale. It was seven acres of wooded land. We had enough money to make a down payment and pay on a five-year land contract in the owners would agree. Walt, the treasurer, was totally opposed to spending money to buy the land. With Jim's leadership and the backing of the other deacons, he was outvoted, and he resigned from the board. This was a blessing in disguise. He would have fought us all through the building program. We had two more treasurers after that. Jane became treasurer and helped us through the entire building program, and she did a fantastic job. And then Colleen became treasurer after we moved into our new building, and she was a tremendous blessing too.

The church had enough money to buy the land or to take me on full time at this point. Jim French wanted me to go full time. The stress of working two full-time jobs and working at the mission was bad enough in itself, and pastoring full time was very demanding. So he asked me about it. I told Jim the church needed to move forward and buy this land. I did not want the church to spend the money on me; it needed to buy the land before someone else did, or the opportunity would be lost. I said the board could reconsider this later after the church was built. The board reluctantly agreed.

We made an offer on the land, and the owners accepted. As we worked to pay the land off, I had to work at the mission for three more years before the church did take me on full time. But they knew this 1.3-million-dollar building program was going to take my full-time attention, so they took me on full time before we actually started to build, thank the Lord.

Before I finished working at the mission, I had the opportunity to switch from third shift and work days in the auto donation program. It was a shift Monday to Friday, 8:00 a.m. to 5:00 p.m. I was a licensed mechanic, and we would fix up all the donated cars that came to the mission, resell them, and put the profits into the mission. One year, we fixed and sold nine hundred cars. Just before I left the mission, the head mechanic—Bill—and John, the administrator of the auto donation program, asked me if I would like to have a vehicle for free from the mission, and I could use it for the church. This was a huge blessing.

Over many years, I have given cars, vans, trucks to people who were needy, and I gave it to them for free. I had just given a pickup truck to a needy family, and God gave me two free vehicles in return. One gift was a 2000 Dodge Caravan that the rescue mission gave me so that I could use it for the church, and another car was given to me by my son-in-law, Dave. It was a 1989 IROC Z28 Camaro with only forty-five thousand miles on it! It had sat for five years, so the fuel injectors were all varnished up; but after I replaced all eight fuel injectors, the car ran like a dream. The point of the story is, you cannot outgive God!

When you give to the Lord, Jesus said in Luke 6:38, "Give and it shall be given unto you, good measure, pressed down, and shaken together, and running over shall men give into your bosom. For with the same measure that you give, it shall be given to you again." I tell this story over and over again to show people that you cannot outgive the Lord!! I have more to tell on this subject later.

Picture of 1989 IROC Z28 Camaro

I took five years to pay off the seven acres, and God supplied every penny. And now we had some money to start our building program. It was approximately 1.3 million dollars to build a church to seat three hundred people with classrooms, a nice kitchen, a fellowship hall, and a paved parking lot of a hundred spaces. I had repeated to the board and the church many times that God would supply every penny for the project. Every board member told me later they did not think it would happen but trusted my leadership in the whole matter.

We had a burn-the-mortgage ceremony, and we started to cut down and remove all the trees/brush from the property. I had been through a building program in Indiana, and I knew the bureaucrats would make us save some trees; and we didn't have a single special tree that needed to be saved. So we cut them all down before I applied for any permits! We lived in the country, so many of the neighbors burned wood in their woodstoves because propane was so expensive out there. I put up a sign, "Free Wood," and the neighbors came from all around us to get the free wood. One family was a Jehovah's Witness family. They got the free wood, started coming to our church, and got saved—praise the Lord!

God sent people to our church that had the talent and abilities to help us build. People had tractors, a front loader, ditch witches, and lots of chainsaws. The women worked right alongside of the men and helped clear the land. We had retired builders, an electrician, and people with many carpenter skills. God was supplying the money and the people to do the work.

I was preaching the books of Ezra and Nehemiah as we built since they both were involved in a building program too. There were many applications I used as we built. And miracles of miracles, we did not have a single major fight over the building program. We did not have a single Baptist brawl. I let the people vote on everything, and whatever the majority voted, that is what we did; God gave us such a spirit of unity—it was wonderful!

Love Thy Neighbor
Better Than Thyself

I lived in the neighborhood where the church was located. I loved my neighbors more than myself. In the houses all around me, I was inviting all the neighbors to church. Their children would come to my house daily, and I gave them ice cream, bread sticks, candy, etc. And I gave them Gospel comic book tracts that are published by Chic Tracts.

The kids and teens loved those tracts. The children and teenagers were getting saved all over my neighborhood. Then the parents would come and get saved and started coming to my church. It was wonderful to see God work. I was like the neighborhood bank. The teens would come and ask me if there were work they could do to earn some money. They stacked my wood, cut my grass, raked my leaved, painted my house, and the little kids would wash my vehicles every Saturday. That loving heart that God gave me was literally poured out into my neighborhood.

One day, there was a family a few houses down from me, and they were quite poor. They ran out of wood in the middle of the winter. Their son helped me with the woodpile in the summer, and their little girl would wash my car every Saturday. So the parents sent the little girl to see me. Here this precious little girl comes down to see me, and she says, "Pastor Dan, we don't have any more wood, and our house is down to fifty degrees. Can we have some wood?"

My heart was so touched with love for this family. I said, "Sure, sweetie, tell your mom and dad to come get some wood." And then I bought her an electric blanket to help keep her warm.

Another family with five children had gotten way behind in their electric bill. They owed nine hundred dollars! So their power had been cut off. Living in the country, you have to have an electric pump to get well water. It was in the middle of July and was very hot. These children had also been to my house many times and had attended our VBS programs and got saved. So they sent Robert, their ten-year-old son, to see me. Nancy said I was a big sucker and couldn't say no to the kids. I don't know if I was a big sucker, but I could never tell these precious children no.

Robert came to my door and said, "Pastor Dan, we don't have any electricity, and no water. Can you help us?"

My heart was just pumping love for this boy and his family. I talked with the mother, got her account number, and called the electric company. They said if I would pay two hundred dollars on a credit card, they would turn the power back on. I paid that amount, and their electricity was turned on again.

Deuteronomy 15:11 says, "For the poor shall never cease out of the land; therefore I command you, saying, 'Thou shall open your hand wide unto thy brother, to the poor, and to the needy in the land.'"

Remember, you cannot outgive God! I didn't always have extra money to help these people, but I lived by the promises of God and gave and gave and gave, and God gave back more than I gave away.

Another neighbor that lived down a dirt road near me had a goat named Gabby. Gabby was a rascal and would climb out of her penned in area and run around the neighborhood. One day, she got loose, and she was running in my yard and was running back and forth across the street. People would drive down our street at sixty miles per hour. I was afraid she was going to get hit by a car. To grab her by the antlers would cause her to go into a fight mode. So I made a lasso out of a nylon rope and lassoed her. Then I tied her to a big oak tree in my front yard, and I figured when my neighbor got home from work, I would get Gabby back home.

Gabby laid there under that tree for about two hours. All of a sudden, she got up and took off full blast. When she got to the end of the rope, it was a sudden jerk on the rope and a dead stop. Her feet went out from under her, and she was lying on her side, shaking her legs, and didn't get up. I figured either she broke her neck, or the rope tightened up and cut off her air supply. I ran outside; sure enough, the nylon rope was so tight she could not breathe. I tried to get my fingers under the rope to get her some air; it was too tight. She stopped moving, eyes rolled up into her head, and her tongue fell out. She was dead!

I ran back into the house and got a sharp knife. I ran out to her, slipped the sharp blade under the rope, cut, and the rope released. She was still not moving—eyes rolled up, tongue hanging out. I didn't want to tell my unsaved neighbor I killed his goat, so I asked the Lord to help me revive the goat. God put in my mind to start pumping the goat's chest. I pushed down hard, *umpa, umpa,* and let up.

Suddenly the goat sucked in a big gasp of air since I had pushed all the air out of her lungs with the compressions, and she opened her eyes and started breathing again. Praise the Lord I brought a goat back from the dead. I never even heard of one of Jesus's disciples ever doing that!

Gabby laid there for about ten minutes, breathing. Then she got up, walked up to my porch, and laid there until the owner came home. I did not tell him what happened. I wasn't sure how he would take all of that, but thank the Lord Gabby was alive!

Building the Kingdom of God

Part 2, Continued

Now let me finish how God did miraculous things to get our church built. I had these two promises from God, and I not only claimed these promises but did so publicly with the people of my church. The Lord had built my faith up strong by now, and the people saw my strong faith in God's promises; they had faith with me. Everything rises and falls on leadership, and God gave me leadership skills necessary to lead this flock. The two promises are Philippians 4:19, "But my God SHALL supply all your needs according to his riches in glory BY Christ Jesus," and John 14:13, "And whatsoever you shall ask in my name, that will I do, that the Father may be glorified in the Son."

I typed up those verses on an eight-and-a-half by eleven-inch sheet of paper. We went over to the cleared seven acres to dedicate the land and the whole building project to God. I read out loud those verses, then I laid the paper on the ground, and I stood on it with both feet and said, "I'm standing on these promises of God. We are not going to the Bank of America. We are going to the bank of God."

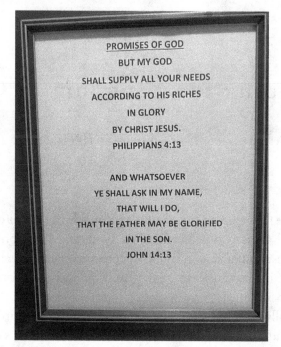

Picture of the two verses used at the dedication

There was a large stump about three feet across where we had cut down an oak tree. It was located right where the new sanctuary would be built. I would go stand on that stump day after day, lift my hands up to heaven, and ask God to bring in the money and build this church right where that stump was located.

God had already moved to get us this far, but more blessings were coming. We needed a contractor. There was no human way I was going to get a contractor for a thousand dollars again. One day, a new man came to visit my church. He was quiet, but he was really thinking. All through the service, I could see he was thinking about something. At the end of the service, he was standing by the front door of the church, and he pointed over to the cleared land. He said, "Are you going to build a new church over there?"

I said, "Yes, we are."

He said, "I'm a contractor, and I own the business. I could build that church for you."

I said, "Great, how much would you charge us?"

He said, "I'll do it for free, no charge."

Praise the Lord! I couldn't believe it, but why should I doubt a miracle when God is in a project? And he did the whole project for free; he did not charge us one penny. He then asked how much money we had so far. I told him we had about $150,000. He figured that would be enough to put up the shell, and it was in part because he wasn't charging us any labor from his company. He did that for free too. He was really blessing us.

So the people took a vote to start, and we would trust God to bring in the rest of the money to compete it. I asked the people to pray for God to give and bless them in a way so that they would have extra money to donate to the building program.

And God did bless the people in so many ways. Money would come in unexpectedly to a family, and they would tithe 10 percent of it to the building fund. In some cases, they gave all the increase that God brought in. One man been saving pennies for twenty years. He had a big water cooler jug, and it was nearly full. He donated the entire jug, and when the bank counted all the pennies, there were thirty-two thousand pennies in the jug! We gave piggy banks to the kids, and they filled them up time and time again and donated the money.

While I had been working at the rescue mission auto shop, there was a retired businessman who would work at the shop two days a week. He enjoyed working on cars, and he did real good work. The Lord laid on his heart to help us. He asked me to never give out his name, so I won't; but over the next three years, he gave over $250,000 dollars. He was our largest single donor. God had allowed his path and mine to cross, and he graciously gave to the Lord!

We had another man give about $225,000 dollars to the building fund. So between them both, they gave over half a million dollars. Praise the Lord! Many people gave of their time to help build the church. Businesses would give us discounts since it was for a new church.

When the project was nearly completed, we needed fifty thousand dollars to finish everything. We put up a large paper thermometer to show as the giving came in. The last amount that came in was sixty-five thousand dollars, which was fifteen thousand dollars more than needed. God kept his promise; he *did* supply all our needs with extra to boot—just like when I needed food in Indianapolis, he gave us food and money overflowing.

Battles Won, Building a Church

But we did have some battles with a few bureaucrats in our building program. Satan opposed our efforts, just like he fought against Nehemiah when he was building the new wall. Our building plans were drawn by an architect that had used the same plans to build another church, which was located in a different township than our church. But the codes and building plans were the same.

So he drew the church building plans without a sprinkler suppression system. But the fire marshal in our township wasn't as agreeable or as workable as the fire marshal in the other township. He insisted that we had to have a sprinkler system in our new church. Because we were in the country, it would require its own well, its own generator, a thousand storage tanks, and all the plumbing. It would cost us an additional three hundred thousand dollars. Now I know God can supply that, but it wasn't necessary. It was unnecessary, according to our architect. But the fire marshal said we had to do it, and if we didn't like his answer, we could sue him.

So my contractor did some refiguring. He figured that if we took two feet off the front of the sanctuary and resubmitted the building plans, we would not have to have a sprinkler system. And sure enough, that worked. We also did not call our kitchen a kitchen on the building plans. We called it a warming room. We did not have an oven, so we didn't need all the requirements like a kitchen would call for in equipment, including a stainless-steel hood and venting system.

The fire marshal told us if he ever came for a surprise inspection and we had an oven in the warming room, he could close us down. This isn't exactly a spirit of cooperation form township officials. But we got through without a lawsuit and without installing a lot of expensive equipment.

Another bureaucrat with an attitude was our drain commissioner. She had just been voted into office and was going to be hard to work with. Our architect said the retention pond was to be a certain size to catch the runoff water from our parking lot. When we submitted the plans to the drain commissioner, she said it had to be twice as large. We asked why, and she said, "Because I said so." That was a real educated answer now, wasn't it? But it's either we do it their way or waste money on a lawyer. We just get it done and keep building.

So we dug out this huge hole in the front of our property for the unreasonable commissioner. We took all the extra dirt and put it up on the spot where the new building was going to sit. As a result of all that extra dirt, it raised the foundation of the building high enough so we did not have to put in a pump-up station for our septic system. Praise the Lord. As a matter of fact, we made the code by an inch!

Now we had another problem with another bureaucrat. This supervisor was the inspector for our septic system and drain field. We put in everything like he said. When we asked for the final inspection so we could cover everything up with dirt, a new supervisor came to inspect. And he said we were told wrong, and the field was in the wrong place. Can you imagine digging up all the drain tubes, stones, etc.? He also said we also had to put in a pump-up station, even though the other inspector said we did not. The pump-up station would cost us about thirty-five thousand dollars.

My contractor asked, "Why the change to have a pump-up station?"

He said it was because he estimated we would use ten thousand gallons of water a month. There was no way we would use that much. We only used the building Sundays and Wednesdays. Our contractor went to the other church that was built like ours and inquired about their water bill. They were on city water, so if we got their water records, we could see how much water was being used with a congregation the size of ours.

When our contractor got the water records, they only used two thousand gallons of water a month. So we prayed as our contractor went back to see this inspector. And he saw the records, changed his mind, and he said we did not need a pump-up station and we could leave the septic system right where it had been placed, praise the Lord.

Satan never did win in any of the obstacles or roadblocks he tried to throw in our way, just like the enemies of Nehemiah never won either.

Project Completed

When we finally finished our building program, the people saw how God did everything. It increased their faith so much. It changed the way they prayed. They were asking God to do some miracles in other situations. They had the faith that nothing is impossible with God. My deacons were even true believers now; they saw with their own eyes what God had accomplished with a mustard seed of faith. My dear elder, Jim French, was able to be there for the dedication Sunday. God had allowed him to live long enough to see the completion.

We had our grand opening celebration in January of 2016. The church would seat three hundred people, and we had 290 people there on that Sunday, praise the Lord.

Picture of Jim French at dedication

Picture of the people at the dedication service

We took the old church building and took out the pews, and we put in an air hockey table, foosball, pool table, Ping-Pong table, and couches and chairs, and made it into a real nice teen center. We had about 40 teenagers that called our church their home church. It was wonderful, praise the Lord. I started with 8 people in that little church building at fifty dollars a week. When I finished the building program, we had 220 people in the church family, and I was now making fifty thousand dollars a year, praise the Lord!

I had now completed forty years of ministry. I went through two stressful building programs, and my work at the mission for ten years had taken its toll. I should have taken a sabbatical along the way, and I was burned out. I decided to retire from full-time ministry for now. So before I left the church, I took a number of steps to make sure the work would continue, and to be successful.

I had the board vote and pass unanimously two very important promises to the congregation. I also had people installed in every program of the church to ensure that the programs would continue and stay strong. The first promise I had the board to vote and pass unanimously was that as soon as I retired, they would have an ordained pastor come from IMI/SOS International and serve as interim pastor to help the church through the transition to get a new pastor and to keep peace and to protect the flock for Satan's devices.

The board not only passed this resolution unanimously but also signed the paperwork with IMI/SOS to get this new interim pastor. It was a signed commitment that the board would accept this interim pastor. I told the people for three months of this agreement.

The second promise/resolution I had the board to vote on was that they would not make any major changes to the church in any way during the interim period. This, again, was to protect the flock because I loved them so much; this was designed to protect the church as well. I told the church for three months about this too, and the church the board agreed and passed both of these promises/resolutions unanimously. The whole church was in agreement with both of these resolutions.

As a good shepherd, I retired from the church with not a single penny of debt owed by the church, and I put in place those two very important resolutions to keep the church strong and protected from the devil's schemes.

The wonderful blessing to me is to see my former sheep, that I still love, are all going to Bible-teaching churches! I am so glad to see they are going forward for the Lord. Many of the members call me, have friended me on Facebook, and talk with me on the phone. I love and miss them all so much! I also interim pastored two Baptist churches since my semi-retirement, and I had so many blessings working with those two churches. I have lifelong friends from them too.

One church in Muskegon that I served as interim pastor just had 194 people attend their Easter cantata. The great lessons of prayer and faith the people saw are not forgotten. The many things the people saw God do will last a lifetime for them and their children who witnessed it all too. God took fifty years of lessons to mold me so that when I was needed to accomplish his plans for my life, I was prepared, equipped by God, and willing to do so.

Earthly Inheritance

Deuteronomy 18:1–2 says, "The Levitical priests, the whole tribe of Levi, are to have no allotment or inheritance with Israel… They shall have no inheritance among their fellow Israelites; the Lord is their inheritance as he promised them."

I have said many times in this book, God always keeps his promises. I never took a ministry based on what it paid. I took a ministry because it was God's will. So I worked for some poor ministries. I was never able to save anything for retirement, so I literally took God at his word again and have trusted him to be my inheritance. I was given a seventy-acre farm. I was given a lakefront home in Florida to retire. I have been given car after car and money over and over again. I have a very loving family that made most of this possible, but it was the Lord that allowed these generous family members to give me an inheritance that I could never have been able to save enough by myself. I am still not fully retired. I am substitute teacher in three Christian schools in Florida. I do pulpit supply and interim ministry in Michigan, and I have just been asked to be an assistant pastor for a pastor in Florida. God is not finished with me yet!

Eternal Inheritance

God has plans for you too, my dear reader. Let God have his way in your life. Let Jesus's love flow from his heart through your heart and into the hearts of others. It will be joy like you never had before! You will see people in heaven because of you.

> And Jesus said, "Lay not up for yourselves treasure upon the earth, where moth and rust doth corrupt, and where thieves break through and steal, but lay up for yourselves treasures in heaven, where neither moth nor rust doth corrupt, and where thieves do not break through nor steal, for where your treasure is there will your heart be also." (Matthew 6:19–20)

Conclusion

The world can be truly transformed by Christ and the love of Christ. When people see that love in a ministry or in the life of a Christian or in the heart of a pastor, they will come. Lives will be changed. We are blood vessels, branches of the vine, the supply line of Jesus's love to others. His heart of love flows through our hearts and into the hearts of others.

> By this shall all men know that you are my disciples, because you love one another. (John 13:35)

> And now abideth faith, hope, charity, but the greatest of these is [agape] love. (1 Corinthians 13:13)

> Only one life, twill soon be past, only what's done for Christ will last. (Charles Studd)

About the Author

Rev. Pastor Dan Smith has been in the ministry for forty-three years, and he has been married for forty-six years. He and his wife, Nancy, have three adult children. He graduated in 1976 with a BA degree in ministry. His ministerial roles have been youth pastor, teacher, Christian school teacher, executive director of Child Evangelism Ministries of Elkhart and LaGrange Counties, rescue mission employee, pastor, and interim pastor.

He was a police chaplain and conducted services for inmates in jail for many years. He has an abundance of stories from his ministerial roles, as well as an abundance of stories from his work in the secular arena. He is currently serving with an interim pastor organization, filling pulpits and helping churches without a pastor. He is also serving in a pastoral role in a local church in Florida.